Viewpoint:
Key to
Fiction Writing

FRANCIS L. FUGATE

Boston   THE WRITER, INC.   *Publishers*

To

MY WIFE ROBERTA

for whom the learning of this

has meant

so many lonely nights

and

a few goodies

CONTENTS

INTRODUCTION

THIS DISCUSSION of fiction writing rests upon the assumption that the writer burns between the desire to tell his story and the desire to have it read. As Emerson put it, " 'Tis the good reader that makes the good book."

Because the first desire is so often easier to fulfill than the second, I approach fiction in this book by way of the techniques of viewpoint, that most vital link between the writer and his reader. In all its facets, viewpoint is truly "a many-splendored thing," reaching from within the writer—from the driving force of his drama—through his characters and his story to the heart and mind of the reader by way of the reader's reason for reading.

Although this book presents techniques and devices pointed toward improving the writer's ability to write good fiction, the art of writing can never be a formalized set of rules. When it is, neither you nor I will any longer be interested in doing it. As a creative art, writing must ever be reaching out beyond today's literary maxims and editorial requirements, and the writer must be forever learning his craft.

During a truly creative process, the artist cannot allow a headful of *do*'s and *don't*s to weaken the force which drives him, yet he must apply the competence of the art in order to be successful. To solve this dilemma, I urge upon the writer a period of honest learning and practice until the ways of writing fiction come to him as a gift, so that he can forget conscious learning. Then he can give himself to his story in his entirety.

Viewpoint:
Key to
Fiction Writing

I

THE WHAT AND WHY
OF VIEWPOINT

———•—•—•———

As a fiction writer you possess only one power over and above the powers of your fellowman. That power is your very reason for being: *You have the ability to live the life of another.* Basically, it is only because of this ability that readers will read your works.

The nonwriter looks at another human and wonders what is going on within his mind, what he is thinking about, how he really feels. The writer does not wonder; he uses his imagination to project himself and find out. The writer's primary function is to supply this information about such people in such situations as readers might like to know. His art is in being able to transport his readers into the heart and mind and body of someone else.

The idea of viewpoint in fiction has been expressed in various ways over the past half century or so: angle of narration, story attitude, narrative method, perspective, focus, obtaining reader identification, vicarious participation, and others. During this time, by the slow distillation of experimentation, trial and error, and reader selection, our knowledge of the subject and its techniques has grown to a respectable body, and the word *viewpoint* is coming into common use to encompass the idea.

We need to be certain that we know the "what" and "why" of viewpoint in order that we may learn the "how" of it. Viewpoint forms the bridge between the heart and mind of the writer and the heart and mind of his reader. It is the writer's means of control over his reader. Without effective use of viewpoint, the writer's meaning and intent may well be lost in his words.

A composite of dictionary definitions settles down to two meanings for *viewpoint:* 1. The place or position from which one views an object, situation, etc.; and 2. An attitude. It is imperative for the fiction writer to realize that *both* of these definitions must be consistently operative in virtually every word he puts to paper.

The facts pertinent to a situation and the people participating in it are of relative unimportance. In communicating with readers, it is the viewpoint from which those facts are presented to the reader that counts. Let's demonstrate this with a situation. First the facts:

It was two o'clock in the morning of a sweltering day. The day before had been Susan Wadlow's twenty-first birthday, and she had received John King's high-school class ring as a symbol of their betrothal. She wore it on a thin gold chain about her neck. A party celebrating their engagement was still in progress.

The party was going on in a room about twelve feet square. A four-hour accumulation of cigarette smoke had formed into an undulating bluish-gray layer above the heads of some eight couples who were seated on the floor watching and listening to John play a guitar and sing.

John, who wanted to be a professional folk singer, was singing to Susan, "Love, love, O heavenly love, love that cannot be denied."

The only light in the room other than the occasional flare of a match was a floor lamp which glared down on John and Susan. He sat on the forward edge of a chair, leaning over his guitar, and she sat on the floor at his feet. The last bottle of a case of Cokes stood lonely in one corner of the case. The others were abandoned about the room or loosely held in the hands of the spectators.

John wore a faded pair of Levis, a T-shirt, and a pair of sneakers. His tousled curly red hair clung to his perspiring forehead in damp ringlets. He alternated between looking at Susan and concentrating on his fingers as they felt out chords on the frets of his guitar.

Susan was looking up at him intently. She moved close enough for his sneakers to touch her and alternated between feeling the ring and running her fingers along the seam of his Levis.

Those are the facts of the situation, untouched by viewpoint—dead, dull, cold facts which a reader would quickly cast aside. Now let's look at those facts in viewpoint, that is *from within the heart and mind of one of the participating characters:*

Susan Wadlow heard Johnny's flickering fingers strum the first chord of "their song," and the night closed in upon her like the beginning of the most beautiful dream in the world. The sounds of the others faded away behind her. Johnny's smile caught the light, like a ray from Heaven through swirling blue clouds, and his glowing red hair became a carelessly tilted halo.

She closed her eyes to hold the dream as it was and fingered the ring that dangled at her throat. His ring! The ring that would be there every second of every day to tell her that they belonged to each other from this day on.

"Until death do us part," she whispered.

"Love, love, O heavenly love, love that cannot be denied."

The words seemed to enter her heart and explode into a great swelling happiness. She moved closer so that his feet would touch her.

When she opened her eyes, Johnny was concentrating on carefully placing his fingers so that he would play their piece just right. Oh, when they heard him sing in Nashville there wouldn't be any doubt about the future! She ran her fingers up the seam of his Levis and felt the warmth of him streaking through her like an electrical charge. He smiled down at her, and she could feel his lips caressing hers. It would always be that way when he sang.

The beautiful chorus echoed and re-echoed through her mind, "O heavenly love . . . O heavenly love."

But there must be at least two sides to a story if it is going to have any dramatic impact. Let's look at this situation from another viewpoint position:

Ben Wadlow flung open the door. He had no trouble finding Susan: There she sat, groveling at the feet of that lazy, hulking, slovenly, good-for-nothing John King. The guitar in his hands throbbed and screamed and pulsed, and Ben could feel the harsh waves of its sound against his eyeballs.

"Love, love, O heavenly love, love that cannot be denied."

Then Ben saw the big ring dangling from a chain around Susan's neck, and its meaning slammed into his body. The stale, hot, smoky air seared his throat as he sobbed, "The age of consent! Oh God!"

There he was, seducing her, in a spotlight right in front of God knows how many people.

Ben saw the scattered bottles. She was drunk, that was what it was. Maybe in the morning when she— Susan clutched the ring to her and looked up at John King, the way she used to look up at Ben, and Ben knew it was hopeless.

By God, he had given her mother an honest-to-God diamond—when he had a job and knew he could support her. "Love, love." The voice grated against his eardrums. John King would never make a cent with that caterwauling.

He saw Susan snuggle up to the filthy tennis shoes and pat John's legs. The voice pierced Ben's skull and the chorus screamed through his mind, "Love that cannot be denied . . ."

A fate worse than death, and there was nothing he could do about it.

Love and courtship, engagement parties, and aspirations to be a folk singer are physiological, sociological, and psychological phenomena which are appropriate to factual narration and precise clinical analysis; but that is not the way we are accustomed to looking at such things when we encounter them either in fiction or in life. In fact, this point should be remembered and repeated every time you, as a fiction writer, find yourself about to be hypnotized by the pure facts of the situation: *There is virtually nothing with which we become involved in this world that we view only from the standpoint of the cold facts surrounding the issue.*

Note that in neither viewpoint approach to the situation surrounding Susan Wadlow and John King are all of the facts used. It matters not one whit to Susan from where she is sitting on her small pink cloud that the room is twelve feet square or that people are lighting matches behind her; they could be shooting Roman candles and she wouldn't know it. It would give an utterly false rendition of the scene from her viewpoint to include such facts, no matter how true or how lifelike they may be.

On the other hand, some "facts" show up in viewpoint which do not exist in the situation: To Ben Wadlow, any would-be folk singer who has just given his daughter a ring would be a hulking lout with a caterwauling voice; such an act would have to have been the result of a drunken orgy. This is an attitude which is inherent in the character of the kind of a father he is. To him, these are very real facts, and for a fiction writer to omit them would be a false portrayal.

Viewpoint is not to be construed as a license for the perversion of truth, the withholding of facts, or willful distortion by the writer. Remember that one of the reader's prime reasons for reading is to find out how another person *really* thinks and feels under a given set of circumstances. It is the writer's task and duty to create the truth as it exists within his viewpoint character to the best of his ability.

Now let's go back to our definition of viewpoint: *The place or position from which one views an object, situation, etc. An attitude.* For your narrative to take on dramatic life, the "one" who views must be a person: a living, breathing, and—above all—feeling and thinking human being. The "place or position" must be within that human being. And the totality of the individual's view must express the singleness of his attitude at that time. So viewpoint becomes a highly selective presentation of highly colored facts as they are experienced by the character who is involved in the situation. When a writer writes "in viewpoint", he communicates his story to his reader from within the very heart, mind, and soul of one of the participating characters.

Earlier I said, "Viewpoint forms the bridge between the heart and mind of the writer and the heart and mind of the reader." In writing fiction, the author creates out of his heart and mind; he uses the viewpoint of his character, his heart and mind, as a catalyst to create an effect in the hearts and minds of his readers.

Notice that I insist upon placing heart before mind. I do this because it is vital for the fiction writer to recognize that both his characters and his readers are controlled more by their hearts than by their minds. This is a fact of life that has created the "why" of viewpoint.

In our daily lives we do not look at the world about us dispassionately as a cold set of facts. We look at the world through the particular set of emotional colored glasses we happen to be wearing at the time. Our attitude toward the world about us is dependent upon the state of our heart at the time we are viewing that "object, situation, etc." of our viewpoint definition. Our view of the same situation may vary as radically from day to day as the reactions of Susan and Ben Wadlow to the engagement party. We excuse such inconsistency of character by saying that we have to be in the mood for this or that.

From the view of the outside observer, such inconsistencies are mysterious and inexplicable. More often than not, they are no less mysterious from the inside, since we do not recognize or take the trouble to trace the complicated inner motivations which control our own actions. The writer cannot be so neglectful. He must know that our feelings and attitudes penetrate our lives so deeply and operate upon us so persistently that we forget they are there.

He must know that we cast votes "for" and "against" on the basis of our emotional attitudes so consistently that politicians have virtually ceased addressing prospective voters on the basis of facts and logic. Instead, the successful politician employs a press agent to create a favorable public image and slants his appeal for votes directly to the hearts of his prospective constituents.

The fiction writer must realize that readers respond to advertising which appeals to them emotionally, not to that which extols the value of a product. He must recognize that much which passes for logic in our lives is after-the-fact justification for decisions which we have made on emotional grounds: After we have decided to buy a new car, not because the old one is worn out but because we want the pleasure and enjoyment which goes with owning a new car, we think up "logical" reasons for trading the old one.

Readers may not want to believe this subservience to their emotions, perhaps because they don't want to admit such frailty. However, they will recognize the truth of it when they meet it in characters in fiction by vicarious participation and an understanding perhaps best described by the word *simpatico*. Much of the writer's art consists in holding a mirror up to mankind's inner nature.

The writer's great trade secret is that he knows how to turn a character inside out, how to make him so real to the reader that the reader knows and understands this paper person better than he knows and understands himself. This is viewpoint.

II

SELECTING YOUR VIEWPOINT
CHARACTER

———•—••—•———

"Every story is somebody's story."

I've heard this truism so many times that I don't know to whom the credit for it should go. For me, the positive value of the statement has been the process of learning its truth, during my own writing and while editing the material which others have written. During that process I have learned enough about myself to enable me to write about others for others.

I firmly believe those five words that begin this chapter are the key to plotting, the most valuable possession a fiction writer—or, for that matter, a nonfiction writer —can own.

It is self-evident that every story worth being called a story must have enough dramatic strength to be told from the viewpoints of most of the participants. Otherwise there would not be sufficient conflict between characters or sufficient motivating force within the characters to provide the story with a reason for being.

Let's run through the character problems involved in a familiar example:

The story of Cinderella could be told through the viewpoint of the stepmother, who had the task of attempting to marry off her unattractive children; it could be told through the viewpoints of the daughters, with the problem of obtaining a husband, each in her own way; it could be told from the viewpoint of the fairy godmother, who was beset by the trials and tribulations of making things come out all right for Cinderella within the limitations of her occult abilities; it could be told from the viewpoint of Cinderella's father, a seldom-heralded soul who obviously needed to whip up enough courage to emerge from his ignoble position in the story's background and speak out in behalf of his own flesh and blood; it could be told from the viewpoint of the king and his problem of finding a suitable mate for his son; it could be told from the viewpoint of the prince, who also had something at stake in the deal.

From any viewpoint other than Cinderella's, the story would be a different yarn from any of the versions of the classic tale with which we are familiar because it would not be Cinderella's story.

The dramatic situation is the vital ingredient of story material. Viewpoint is the lifeline of reader interest. In any dramatic situation, the problem of the leading character will change with a change in the viewpoint approach to the situation. As the viewpoint changes, the sympathy of the reader will change; and each version will make its natural appeal to a different group of readers.

The Cinderella story started so far back in time that its origins are lost in the misty beginnings of mythology. A Cinderella is to be found in virtually every people's folklore. Before the dawn of the printed word, storytellers told of such a character to help sustain the despairing listener who found his situation hopeless, with no apparent way out; his only hope was to have faith that everything would come out all right—and, sure enough, the fairy godmother came along in one form or another.

The natural appeal of this story in all of its versions and variations is to those who look to "fairy godmothers" for solutions to their problems. They recognize the Cinderella character immediately and understand the motivation for his or her faith; they identify with very little prompting.

However, Cinderella has her detractors. For example, there is the Sly Fox. This is a direct descendant of Reynard the Fox of fable fame. The Sly Fox type firmly believes that everybody in the world is out to get the best of him by scheming, and the only way to get ahead is to out-scheme the other schemers. Obviously, this sort of person sets no store by fairy godmothers and has no patience with someone so stupid as to depend upon faith alone to work out his problems.

The Sly Fox, therefore, is not a natural reader for the Cinderella story. He would, however, understand the homely daughter who attempted to outwit the king's herald by cutting off a bit of her heel so that she could jam her foot into the slipper. That girl had wits enough to try to do something about her situation! She'd likely have gotten away with it, too, if it hadn't been that the herald happened to see the blood oozing out of the shoe as they were heading for the palace. A gal with that much nerve deserved another chance.

Later we will discuss the use of viewpoint in making a character appeal to an unfriendly or alien reader. Let it suffice at this point to say that, no matter how massive the mass appeal, no writer has ever been able to appeal to all readers with a single story and will not be likely to in the future.

This diversity of human nature which expresses itself in reader interest provides the reason why every story has to be somebody's story. If a writer were to attempt to tell the Cinderella yarn from several viewpoints in the same story, the effect would be chaotic. At the beginning, the Cinderella fans would naturally identify with Cindy, her problem and her approach to it. They would no sooner be settled comfortably into the viewpoint of someone they could understand than they would find themselves exposed to the problem of the stepmother, her homely children, or somebody else. It would be like purchasing tickets to a symphony concert and discovering that the orchestra's performance was only a short prelude to a wrestling match.

Those readers naturally interested in the stepmother's or her daughters' problems would never get that far in the story. As soon as they found Cinderella, they would leave her sitting in the ashes in the corner of her fireplace and turn to brighter pages.

So in approaching a potential story, the first question the writer must ask himself is, "Whose story am I telling?" In other words, from among all of the characters involved in the situation, which *one* has the most dramatic problem?

Sometimes the writer's nature leaves him no choice. Sometimes he can feel and project his story from only one character's viewpoint. The very reason for the story is that the writer wants to "live" a particular person's life onto paper.

Other times, for example, in the case of a writer who is intimately acquainted with a historical background, the decision may be much more difficult to make. A dramatic situation evolving out of a great social movement can offer so many sympathetic participants that the writer may be tempted to lose the impact of the story by trying to tell about all of the people, rather than penetrating the reader by letting him experience the situation through a single participant.

Not infrequently, the only way to find the answer to the viewpoint question is to test several viewpoint approaches and finally find the right one. Occasionally this dark cloud of labor has a greenback lining: The writer discovers that he has written not one story but two or more, perhaps completely different except for the names of the characters, and probably for completely different markets.

It is well to solve this viewpoint problem during the

plotting stage of a yarn. It is considerably less work to synopsize a story through the separate viewpoints of three or four characters than it is to write a full-blown manuscript from each viewpoint, coming out with three or four first drafts only one of which will be potentially salable.

In selecting a viewpoint character through which to portray a situation, we are selecting the somebody of the story who is going to share his feelings and thoughts with the readers during their participation in the situation. If the resulting work is to be a success, this cannot be an arbitrary selection made from outside the writer; nor can it be a coldly calculated selection. The writer must project himself into a viewpoint which he can feel to be truly the "I" of the story, regardless of the narrative approach he may use.

Normally, the most dramatic character for the portrayal of any situation is the individual who endures the greatest emotional wear and tear or, as some have put it, the "chief sufferer." However, there will be considerable difference of opinion among writers as to who should be the hero or heroine of any given situation. We ticked off half a dozen possible approaches to the Cinderella story other than Cinderella's. Without a doubt, if this story idea were to occur independently to a hundred different writers, all types of viewpoints would be represented in the resulting stories they wrote. In each case the principal character would be the chief sufferer.

There are four major ways in which faulty viewpoint selection and treatment can mar your story. Each of these difficulties can haunt a story from the first word the writer puts on paper until he gives it up or finally files the battered, mail-worn manuscript away. But since these difficulties, arising from faulty viewpoint selection, are obvious from the moment the writer decides which viewpoint to use, he can save himself the frustration and the wasted time that go along with creating page after page of spineless, directionless copy, if he recognizes and heeds the characteristic danger signals.

1. *Events overpower character conflict.*

If you find on approaching a story idea that you are greatly interested in the happenings but simply can't seem to make the thing crystallize through a single viewpoint, you need to take a searching look at the dramatic qualities of the situation. It may be that the situation—at least as you conceive it at that moment—is too anecdotal in nature, that it really does not have the internal character conflict and the protagonist-antagonist relationship necessary to make good dramatic fiction. One warning sign of this is finding yourself trying to step into the narrative with philosophical authorial comment which points up the hidden significance of the happening, *à la* de Maupassant or O. Henry.

2. *Author cannot identify with character.*

Or the difficulty may be that you haven't found the basic conflicts of the situation. This can happen when you become interested in a series of events but, for whatever reason, cannot identify with any of the participants well enough or penetrate him sufficiently to find out what his problems are, why he is as he is. You may find yourself tending to be standoffish and analytical of your characters.

This happens rather frequently when one is attempting to write about an age group different from his own, particularly a considerably younger age group. It may be caused by a Freudian antagonism toward your character. Whatever the reason, you can be assured that if you—the creator of a character—cannot identify with that character well enough to understand him and feel with him, you have small chance of making a reader sympathetic.

You may need to reevaluate your approach to the situation and, consequently, your selection of a viewpoint character. Approach from another viewpoint may reveal conflicts which are more in keeping with your attitude toward the situation.

3. *Seed of story does not stem from
   character involvement.*

A kissing cousin of the above difficulty occurs when you are visualizing a story from its ending, for example an ironic reversal. Unless you "live" your way through the entire chain of events of the situation with somebody who participates in that ending to learn what happened to him to make him act as he did, to build the capacity for the reversal as a part of his character, you have the possibility of arriving at the nub of your story with characters who are every bit as lifeless as the ubiquitous traveling salesman and farmer's daughter of the smoking room stories. In other words, from beginning to climax to ending you must proceed through your story in viewpoint.

This same difficulty can occur when the stimulus of a story is one big scene. The writer cherishes that scene; he builds it in his mind. Then he rushes it onto paper. Within himself he has created its reason for being into a reality. It has become so real to him that he takes it for granted that the reader will feel the same. But on paper, the writer arrives at the scene without having involved the main participant sufficiently to make his actions seem plausible to the reader.

To the reader, the result is comparable to tuning in on the climactic scene of a television program: Some strange people seem to be all worked up about something, but he doesn't know what.

In the case of the big scene, the writer usually has trouble with his ending. More often than not, having spent himself on the big scene, he will then skid to a stop without really bringing his story to a conclusion.

If you find yourself itching to write one scene or chapter that is well along in your story or novel before you do anything else, you may have this problem. The solution is to show your character's involvement in the situation from the beginning of the story. This will almost inevitably provide the necessary motivation for his actions.

4. *Story message overpowers character participation.*

It is obvious that the writer must become wrought up over his story in order to tell it with the depth of feeling which generates dramatic power. Herein can lurk a prime danger. The writer's feelings may be generated by the message he wants his story to convey, rather than by the experiences of the participants in the situation he is planning to use as a vehicle.

This can result in a narrative which degenerates into a propagandistic, tract-like production which would be more appropriate to the editorial columns of a strong-minded newspaper or to a church pulpit than to pages which purport to be fiction. The only cure for this difficulty is to imbed yourself in your story as a participant and live through it from the plotting stage to the final page of finished copy. Make certain that the conflicting social forces—all of them, not just yours—are represented by living, feeling, breathing, acting characters. Dramatic fiction makes a persuasive propaganda medium when artfully presented, and viewpoint is the key to the art.

It is well to remember that the stronger you feel about a cause, the more experience—vicarious or otherwise—you have had to bring you to your present state of feeling. If you simply rant and rave about how you feel, you are merely telling the reader about it. If he already agrees with your attitude, he may read along because he has found a kindred soul; if he does not already agree, he will not read far. On the other hand, if you project yourself into the experience and sufferings of someone who is in the process of arriving at your present state of feeling about the cause, you are *showing* your reader how you came to feel as you do. More people believe what they are shown than will believe what they are told, so by showing your reader you have a fighting chance of winning new converts to your cause.

The chief sufferer of a situation is sometimes elusive. For example, a man might be struck by an automobile and knocked unconscious, undergoing great physical injury; but in his unconscious state he would not be experiencing either physical or emotional reactions. However, his wife could be looking on, physically unhurt but enduring a lifetime of emotional stress. Her reaction could have dramatic value; his could have none, because in his unconscious state there could be no reaction from his viewpoint.

Emotional wear and tear is the prime coin of the dramatic art; physical suffering or its prospect is only one of many possible stimuli. The characters in some of the greatest stories have not suffered physically. Except for rheumatism, Maître Hauchecome, in de Maupassant's "A Piece of String," did not endure a moment of physical pain. His suffering was in the mental and emotional agony caused by his vanity.

Such analysis is an after-the-fact critical process, in many cases accomplished unconsciously by the reader or editor. It is an "I like" or "I don't like" decision: The end result from the reader's or the editor's standpoint is that the story is either effective or ineffective.

If the writer becomes conscious of the causative forces which create his drama, he can greatly increase the effectiveness of his writing.

I am not advocating that the writer kill his creative process by kowtowing to the reader or by attempting to analyze reader reaction as he writes. This will result in the death of the writer's idea with pedestrian prose serving as pallbearer. I do advise the writer to pause at various stages of his work to judge whether he is presenting his idea as effectively as possible.

Story inception is a sort of "blinding flash" which creates within us the seed of an idea. Seldom can we point back to the precise spot in time, space, and thought at which it originated. However, as we progress from seed to idea to story, we can delineate the stages of the process: We get the idea. We think about it, emotionally and/or intellectually, as we evolve an attitude or feeling toward the idea. We find—or become —the people who are to represent it to the reader. . . . We evolve a "plot," mentally or on paper. . . . We write a first draft. . . . We revise. . . . And we write again . . . perhaps again . . . and again. . . . And we come up with a final draft. . . .

The dots are simply the points where the writer should pause to evaluate the way he is expressing his idea, perhaps in terms of the effect on his readers. He should never distort the truth as he sees it; that is the way of hacks.

In the vast majority of cases, the web which entangles the reader is made up of a combination of the internal conflicts, the thoughts, and the feelings of the viewpoint character. The mere events, logically evolved from situation and character as they must be, are only stimuli to make your people worth reading about.

As you approach the seed of your story, you have to answer the question, "In whose feelings, sufferings, and emotions will I have the best chance of penetrating the hearts and minds of my readers?" The right answer to this question will make the seed burgeon and grow. The wrong answer will cause it to shrivel and die.

III

SELECTING YOUR VIEWPOINT

———·•◆•·———

After the writer has selected the character through whom he will tell the story, his problems are just beginning. The real difficulty in using this golden key to narration is in giving proper treatment to the viewpoint once it has been selected. There are several methods of narration, or viewpoints which can be used. The most common are:

1. third person, subjective
2. third person, objective
3. first person, subjective
4. first person, objective
5. second person, subjective
6. omniscient viewpoint

All of these viewpoints have particular adaptabilities and uses which the writer can turn to his advantage. Each places definite limitations upon how the writer can tell his story. Unwitting confusion of two or more will almost invariably lead to loss of story impact. Selection of one for use must not be made as a haphazard choice.

To illustrate the adaptabilities and limitations of these various approaches, I have taken a brief incident in the life of a rather stuffy gentleman named Sir Cedric Banner, a member of the Westchester Club and a thorough adherent to all of its traditions.

Third person, subjective

Sir Cedric Banner settled into his chair, the one vacated only last year when his father died, and picked up his copy of the *Times* from the table at his elbow. It was an uncut copy, just as his father had received the *Times* for fifty years before him. And in spite of the radical young bounders in the Westchester Club with their gaudy slick magazines, Sir Cedric intended to maintain the tradition of reading the *Times* before dinner.

He unfolded the newspaper and took up his paper-knife to slit the as yet unopened sheets. A pleasant warmth seeped through him at the realization that he —he alone, Sir Cedric Banner—was almost single-handedly upholding the club's traditions. As the rich tang of fresh printer's ink wafted up about him, he reflected that there were few there in the commons who had ever smelled it. He glanced up toward Sir Christopher Calvert, whose chair was next to his. He would let Calvert smell the paper, let him see the unslit sheets. Perhaps the young jackass would get some idea of his responsibilities if he saw the proper thing.

But Calvert was turned the other way, reading one of those damnable magazines. Sir Cedric leaned forward out of his chair to look at its title. He froze in mid-air. *Lurid Confessions!* Shades of Queen Bess! Hasn't the idiot any sense at all? Sir Cedric knew what his father would have done. Pater would have snatched the magazine and hurled it into the fireplace. Well, perhaps if one were that old it was all right, but Sir Cedric had always thought violence a bit degrading.

He settled back into his chair and took a good whiff of *Times* ink to quiet the anger that was fermenting within him, burning his cheeks and making the newspaper tremble in his hands. Carefully and deliberately he laid the paper aside, got up, and walked to Calvert's chair. Gently but firmly, he touched his shoulder.

"I say, Sir Christopher, I do hope you were discreet about bringing that thing in here. The porter is an awful gossip, you know."

He managed to keep his voice at that cool impersonal level which is so effective with a reprobate.

With the third person, you maintain the distance which the use of *Sir Cedric, he,* and *him* connotes, allowing your character to parade before your reader; but with the subjective side of the approach you also get the intimacy of being inside your character's mind and body so that your reader can participate vicariously in his emotions and know his most personal thoughts. In other words, your reader is—to a certain extent— looking at your character and at the same time is being imbued with his emotions and feelings: the reader is as one with your character.

The third person, subjective, is the most commonly used viewpoint approach in both fiction and nonfiction. It allows the author maximum control over his story and at the same time gives him control over his readers' minds and feelings. With this approach, the writer can, *if the necessity of his plot dictates,* shift to the viewpoint of another character—provided that the shift is carefully made. It should be noted, however, that indiscriminate shifting from one viewpoint to another will confuse the reader. If the reader does not become mixed up while trying to keep track of who is doing what, to whom and when, he may lose interest in the principal character's problem because of exposure to the problems of other characters. Each time you shift the angle of narration from one viewpoint to another, you weaken the emotional impact and/or sympathy in your reader for your character.

With the third person, subjective approach, the writer can take in the greatest possible swath of a potential reading audience: Those who sympathize with Sir Cedric, those who are perhaps just as stuffy as he is, will go along with him in the story, feeling for him and with him; those who are not capable, by their very natures, of sympathy with such a character can watch the play take place before them with an adequate understanding of the principal character.

This manner of telling does not have the egotism or familiarity of the first person, which can be annoying to a reader who does not identify with the character. The third person allows the writer to employ a sufficiently dignified style to demand respect without seeming inconsistent in the characterization.

On the other hand, use of the third person, subjective, allows the author to emulate the manner of speech or vernacular his character would naturally use in the process of talking and thinking, since the entire story comes through the mind of the viewpoint character, permeated with his thoughts and his reactions to the situation about him and to the other characters in the story. The use of the viewpoint character's natural language to flavor the narration adds to the illusion of reality created by the story and sharpens the characterization.

Strictly speaking, when you are "in viewpoint," a character cannot see himself unless he is in front of a reflective surface. (Perhaps you have noted how frequently characters find themselves in front of mirrors or plate glass windows, particularly in the women's magazines, when the time comes to describe their clothing or physical appearance to the readers.)

Your character not only cannot see himself; he cannot see most of his actions. He cannot see his face get red; he must feel within himself the emotion which causes the heat, embarrassment or anger perhaps. But when you as the writer say "Sir Cedric was angry," or "Sir Cedric felt angry," you are simply telling the reader of a state-of-being, coldly and without emotional impact. Your character is not feeling and your reader cannot identify with a feeling the character does not experience. To write of anger you must know and feel the heat of anger.

The ideal in viewpoint is not telling what emotions Sir Cedric felt, or even how Sir Cedric felt in that emotional state, but making the reader feel the way Sir Cedric does. This effect is comparatively difficult to achieve, but the result is well worth the rewriting it may require.

By pure logic, your character cannot do something

"unconsciously"; if he were unconscious of doing it, he would not know that he was doing it. He may, of course, become aware that he is doing or has done something—as happens to us in real life—and then realize that he was doing it unconsciously.

You must be on guard against such things as "Sir Cedric was genuinely sorry for Calvert as he watched Chris cowering in the corner, his hands clammy with fear." That is an example of slipping into the viewpoint of another character when one should not be there. Certainly it sounds ridiculous. You cannot simply look at someone else and feel his cold, clammy hands. But every writer lets similar slips of viewpoint creep into his early drafts, slips which are not as obvious, perhaps, but which are almost equally devastating to the effect upon the reader if they are not eliminated.

Your viewpoint character cannot properly get into the mind of another character in the story to know what that other character is thinking. He can surmise from the other character's appearance and actions and words, but he cannot be certain. This is frequently an advantage to the writer in maintaining suspense, and, more important, is a reflection of the reality of life.

It is equally easy to slip out of viewpoint in another way. "Sir Cedric had made up his mind: He was determined to end this magazine reading once and for all. The determination was written across the rippling muscles of his broad back as he raised his cane over Calvert's head." Obviously, one cannot see his own back.

If you have never consciously attempted to control viewpoint in writing or have never paid close attention to it, you will probably experience some difficulty in expressing the common everyday emotions from within a character's mind and body, and, therefore, in communicating them to your reader. Most of the time in the first draft stage you should simply feel and write. But it is well to get into the habit of pinpointing your character's emotional state when rewriting. If you discover that you—as the creator—cannot quite identify the emotional state of your character, you can be sure that the confusion will be multiplied in your reader to whom you are attempting to transfer that unidentified emotional state.

It is well to observe yourself in various emotional states to determine exactly how you feel, think, and act, particularly when under stress. If you keep a journal or a notebook and pay particular attention to recording your personal feelings, you will crystallize many rich emotional experiences for future use. In time this will clarify the motivations of your characters immeasurably. Character motivation is a prerequisite to either reader identification or reader understanding; it is perhaps the most important service performed by the use of viewpoint.

If at first you experience difficulty in staying in viewpoint, you can cure that trouble by writing your material originally in the first person and then changing the *I*'s to *Sir Cedric*'s or *he*'s and making other alterations which are necessary. There is usually, however, a considerable difference between the style of writing in the third person story and the intimacy of approach in the first person, as we will shortly see.

Third person, objective

Sir Cedric Banner entered the common room of the Westchester Club and walked directly to his chair. He seated himself as if the chair and the area about it were personal possessions, and well he might since nothing but the bottom of a Banner had touched that chair's seat for more than a half century. As he reached for his copy of the *Times* from the table at his side he seemed to be looking up and over every member of the Westchester Club. Sir Cedric's *Times,* its pages uncut to show that it had not been opened since leaving Fleet Street, was one of the few traditions remaining at the club since the younger members had taken to magazines. Sir Cedric's manner as he unfolded the paper was ample testimony that he deplored the situation.

He picked up his paperknife and started to slit the pages, then seemed to think better of it. A little pleased-with-himself smile broke out as he sniffed at the newspaper. He put aside the knife and started to get out of his chair in the direction of Sir Christopher Calvert. Then he stopped in a half-up half-down crouch, as though paralyzed.

For an instant his face went white, then turned red. He gazed sternly at Sir Christopher's copy of *Lurid Confessions* for an interminable time, considering that his suspended position defied the law of gravity.

Then he dropped back into his chair. His hands were trembling as he moved the *Times* in front of his face, sort of fanning himself. Somehow it seemed to dissipate the anger and his hands ceased to tremble; the red faded from his face. Then he got up out of the chair, advancing his chin before him. Without looking at Sir Christopher, he fastened his gaze on the magazine and tapped the young man on the shoulder.

"I say, Sir Christopher, I do hope you were discreet

about bringing that thing in here. The porter is an awful gossip, you know." His tone was a cold but vibrant echo of the club's past tradition.

In the third person, objective, approach to viewpoint you maintain a reserved distance by the impersonality of *Sir Cedric, he,* and *him.* You have the additional and considerably more potent impersonality of not being within the character's mind and body. More often than not when using the third person, objective, you will actually be narrating from the viewpoint of another character in the story who is seeing the character under consideration. It may or it may not fit your story purpose to let the mind of your viewpoint character reflect upon or interpret your objectively viewed Sir Cedric.

You are under definite limitations when approaching a character in the third person, objective: You cannot put your reader inside his mind; your reader will know only so much of his thoughts and feelings as can be interpolated from his appearance, speech, or actions. In the case of a viewpoint character objectively observing another character, the viewpoint character may make an erroneous assumption. This is as it is in real life, and it may be an important factor in your plot line.

If the story has a viewpoint, the writer cannot properly step out of that viewpoint to tell about or analyze a character who is being treated objectively. Such a character must be conveyed to the reader by his appearance, actions, and speech; by reports of others, and such other objective methods as the particular plot restrictions allow. But, as was mentioned previously, this can be a definite advantage to the story's suspense.

If you are in the mind of Sir Henry What's-His-Name, narrating from his viewpoint and observing Sir Cedric, you are not obligated to tell the reader what is going on in Sir Cedric's mind. Sir Henry can draw the wrong conclusion, or he may simply remain ignorant of Sir Cedric's thoughts and feelings. For an example of the advantage of this, let us say that in the twisting of the plot it develops that Sir Cedric Banner was really envious of Sir Christopher Calvert because the latter did not have the responsibility of upholding Westchester Club traditions. The story is to gain its suspense from the reader's not knowing exactly what Sir Cedric will do in his big moment; the story will make its point by Sir Cedric's reversal of character. In Sir Henry's viewpoint, or any viewpoint other than Sir Cedric's, you do not have to cheat the reader by not showing Sir Cedric's envy; this revelation is saved to provide suspense and surprise.

Don't forget, however, that the reader must not be unfairly surprised. You must put in proper plants so that the reader can look back and say "I should have known that was going to happen." Unless you take this precaution, you will produce a "contrived" story. In other words, your story will have the appearance of something which has been "made up" by a writer, rather than something which has happened that the writer is telling about. It will not have that all-important illusion of reality.

As you tell a story in the third person, subjective, through the viewpoint of your hero, your villain will be handled in the objective, serving as a stimulus and an obstacle to your hero. Faulty handling of viewpoint in portraying this relationship can lead to a serious loss of reader impact. Remember that any time you shift into the villain's viewpoint you are going to motivate him for a great many readers and he will not appear so terrible after all. For example, you consider a man who has stolen to be a criminal—morally and legally— until you discover that he was stealing because his poor old mother would die unless he obtained money in a hurry; then you cease to think of him as morally liable for his criminal act.

The writer should never forget the potential power of his medium. As a matter of history, documented by legislative act and court decision during the past half century, Western civilization has been trending away from traditional concepts of right and wrong (The student of viewpoint might ask, "Traditional concepts from whose viewpoint?") to indulge ethical codes which have been derived by emotional processes. This has been brought about by reversing the traditional viewpoint approaches to moral issues. Fiction has had its part in bringing about the changes, and certainly it has served in holding up its mirror to history.

It is possible to tell a story in which you approach every character in the third person, objective. However, you had better have an excellent reason for doing so, because this viewpoint approach virtually nullifies any possibility of reader identification with a character. Instead of your story being somebody's story, it is nobody's story.

Shirley Jackson's little gem called "The Lottery" * is such a story. The author did not go into the mind of a single character in the story, and for an excellent technical reason. If she had, she would have been bound by that unwritten agreement between the writer and the reader to reveal that the people involved in the event she was portraying were holding a drawing to determine which of them would be stoned to death by the others. If the reader knew this, the story would lose its shock effect. Had this story been narrated in the third person, subjective, it would have been an entirely different yarn, perhaps about the reaction of someone to the possibility of being stoned to death, or some other facet of the affair.

Incidentally, read "The Lottery" and note the superb manner in which the author made a villainess out of one character—Mrs. Hutchinson—simply by portraying that character's objective actions and words, but managed to do this without letting even the cat's tail protrude from the proverbial bag.

Except for its uses in nonfiction or in a special story situation such as occurs in "The Lottery," the third person, objective, treatment is in almost every case used with the third person, subjective. The two viewpoints

* Originally published in *The New Yorker*, 1948, this story is available in several anthologies.

are virtually inseparable. However, it is vital that the writer know the difference between these two third-person approaches. We have already noted the difficulties of treating a character objectively when the narration should be taking place within his mind, and vice versa. An indiscriminate mixture of the two approaches will lead to confusion and loss of dramatic impact for the story.

The third person, objective, permits an analytical treatment of character, and herein hides one of its deepest and most artfully concealed pitfalls. If the approach is purely objective, the writer is sorely tempted to analyze each and every character by use of author comment. The average writer of no matter how much experience has an almost overpowering urge to play psychologist; this desire more often than not gets the best of his story.

From one of his character's viewpoints, the writer can make an analysis of other characters. However, for the sake of plausibility, the writer must make certain that such an analysis is within the capabilities of his viewpoint character, that the analysis is not the writer's words and knowledge put into the character's mouth and mind. In order to talk and think like a practicing psychiatrist, your character must be a practicing psychiatrist in the story.

First person, subjective

I headed for the common room of the Westchester Club and my *Times*. The hour before the before-dinner sherry is about the only peaceful time left, now that the

young boors have taken over with their eternal yam-
mering. I don't think they actually respect the hour and
what it can do for one's digestion; I think it's their
craving for those damnable slick magazines. At any rate,
the quiet gives a man time for thought and goes a piece
toward maintaining tradition.

I went to my chair—for more than fifty years a
Banner has occupied that chair—and picked up my
Times, uncut, you know; that's the way Father always
got it. Not only is it a mark of distinction to slit your
own paper, but it keeps the blooming servants out of it.
And the smell of fresh ink! That's the wonderful part
of it.

I was about to slit the paper when it occurred to me
to let Sir Christopher Calvert smell the ink. It would be
an excellent excuse to let the upstart younker see that
somebody is still keeping up the Westchester tradition.

I had just risen from my chair when I saw the magazine Calvert was reading. It was like a slap in the face.
Lurid Confessions, if you'll believe it. I went hot all
over. Only by the grace of God did I control myself
sufficiently to keep from snatching the magazine from
his hands and flinging it into the fireplace. That is what
the Pater would have done. However, that is also what
young Calvert would have done—in anger, not in
righteous wrath. He wouldn't understand the difference
between the two.

Only by sitting still and taking good deep whiffs of
the *Times* did I calm myself enough to approach Calvert. I didn't even look at him; I looked at the magazine. I tapped him on the shoulder, just hard enough
for him to know it wasn't friendly but not hard enough
to be offensive.

"I say, Sir Christopher, I do hope you were discreet
about bringing that thing in here. The porter is an
awful gossip, you know."

I managed it without a tremble in my voice. I kept it low and cold, with just a touch of fury.

Here again we are inside Sir Cedric's mind and body. The *I*'s, *me*'s, and *my*'s of the first person make for the most intimate approach. You, as the writer, can live your character's way through the story, feeling and thinking and speaking for him; you have the opportunity to place him very close to the reader, to achieve the maximum of reader identification. The first person, subjective, viewpoint focuses a microscope on the character's mind and feelings and shows his every motivation, revealing his most secret thoughts, and making his inner emotions a part of the reader's imagination.

To be plausible, the first-person story must be told in the vernacular of the character—or at least in a way which gives the illusion of his manner of speaking. Beware of dialect; for the majority of readers it is so difficult to read that it is virtually taboo in many magazines. And a too-realistic first-person approach to the character by way of his stream of consciousness makes for a rambling discourse, using too many words without producing a sufficient measure of sustained action and dramatic impact.

Remember that the prime purpose of your storytelling is to show a character reacting to a situation or to another character. You may have a fine style, a wonderful facility with words, but those words stand a much better chance of being read if they all have a bearing upon the story you promise to tell your reader. In real

life, thoughts and conversations are disconnected, repetitive, and horribly rambling. In writing, we must
create an illusion of reality without being long-winded
and boring. A highly realistic approach to a character's
manner of thinking or expression might be praised
for its realism. But in telling a story you should not
draw attention to the style. In doing so you let your
readers escape from the grip of your story; you sacri-
fice the very thing you are offering for sale. A comparatively small part of the reading audience reads for
writing style alone.

The first person, subjective, imposes stringent restrictions upon what the writer can do. He can tell no
more than his character can see, hear, feel, and think.
If your plot demands that the reader have information
which absolutely cannot be available to your viewpoint character, you will have to change either the entire viewpoint or the plot of the story. Having committed yourself to a first-person approach, you cannot
shift to another viewpoint within the narrative.

There are certain weaknesses inherent to first-person
narration. If your yarn concerns a character who has
done great deeds of daring, in using the first-person
approach, you run the risk of creating an egotistical
braggart whom a majority of readers will find unsympa-
thetic. It never seems quite modest, either in fiction or
in real life, for a truly great or a truly brave man to
say "I . . . I . . . I . . ." If the deeds of daring are of
such a nature that they would seem implausible, you
have to do some real finagling in the first person,
subjective, to obtain the advantage of the testimony of

other characters to your hero's feats. The effect usually seems contrived.

There are many outstanding examples to prove that it can be done and be done well, but the average writer has a great deal of difficulty in sustaining a first-person narrative over a considerable length of wordage. As the length increases, the repetitive *I* becomes more and more monotonous, the character's emotional state mounts higher and higher, and his weeping and wailing waxes more melodramatic. The confessions, of course, are completely first-person, subjective. They must reach a high emotional pitch to achieve impact upon their particular reading audience. The confession magazines, incidentally, provide an excellent medium for the writer to study the limitations of the first person, subjective.

All characters in the story other than the hero or heroine become "objects" to which the leading character reacts. The treatment of these characters must be objective; their impact upon the leading character must motivate subjective reactions. The greater the emotional reaction the more melodramatic the story tends to be. This viewpoint approach offers little opportunity to give your reader relief from a long-sustained emotional state. You cannot lead your reader to an emotional crest, give him a bit of a breather (perhaps by the use of background or atmosphere), and then take him to a higher crest without giving the impression that during the interim your character's problem has ceased to be of importance. Everything in your story must contribute to an emotional reaction in your reader. If it

doesn't, your story will be implausible and reader interest will sag.

It is well to look carefully at your plot before you
embark upon narration in the first person, subjective.
That look may save you much rewriting or having to
put a story aside because it simply will not jell in the
viewpoint which you have selected for the telling.

One question comes up rather frequently: "How
about shifting from third person, subjective, to first
person, subjective, and back again?" Fine—*if* you can
get away with it, *if* it comes off smoothly and communicates to the reader without having the device
attract attention to itself. Normally, this is done most
successfully when you are deep in your character's
viewpoint, and the first-person portion is more like
thoughts (expressed mentally) without quotation marks
than a shift to the viewpoint character as a narrator:

> Sir Cedric resumed his seat and watched Calvert
> reading his copy of *Lurid Confessions* as unconcernedly
> as if it were a respectable periodical. [The next thing
> you know, he'll be wanting me to post it for approval
> on the Westchester subscription list; and the sad thing
> is that there are enough of the young bounders to vote
> it in.] The helpless frustration started the aching in his
> stomach again, and Sir Cedric returned to the soothing
> stability of his *Times*.

The brackets are used merely to identify the first-
person passage. Many times such "quoted" thoughts
are italicized. This helps the reader identify them. The
use of italics rather than quotation marks keeps quoted

thoughts from being confused with actual quotations of spoken words. However, it should be pointed out that the use of too many italics can also become confusing; excessive italicization is not particularly good from a style standpoint.

Actually, the transition from third person, subjective to first person, subjective is by no means a new idea. Charles Dickens, one of the earliest experimenters with viewpoint, tried it more than a century ago. In *Bleak House,* he alternated between third and first person; the novel was not one of his best works. In *A Tale of Two Cities,* Dickens used a shift to the first person and to the present tense in an attempt to give dramatic immediacy to the climactic flight of the Darnays from Paris. First, from a conventional third person, past tense narrative, he shifted to the present tense and then to first person:

> As the patient eyes were lifted to his face, he saw a sudden doubt in them, and then astonishment. He pressed the work-worn, hunger-worn young fingers, and touched his lips.
>
> "Are you dying for him?" she whispered.
>
> "And his wife and child. Hush! Yes."
>
> "O you will let me hold your brave hand, stranger?"
>
> "Hush! Yes, my poor sister; to the last. . . ."

> The same shadows that are falling on the prison are falling, in the same hour of that early afternoon, on the Barrier with the crowd about it, when a coach going out of Paris drives up to be examined.
>
> "Who goes here? Whom have we within? Papers!"
>
> The papers are handed out and read.

· · ·

"The road is clear, my dearest. So far, we are not pursued."

Houses in twos and threes pass by us, solitary farms, ruinous buildings, dye-works, tanneries and the like, open country, avenues of leafless trees.

.   .   .

The wind is rushing after us, and the clouds are flying after us, and the moon is plunging after us, and the whole wild night is in pursuit; but, so far, we are pursued by nothing else.

It is out of such experimentation that our present knowledge of the use of viewpoint has been distilled. Today, such shifting either of viewpoint or tense by experienced writers is comparatively rare, more because superior techniques have been developed than because of any established conventions of style.

First person, objective

I was waiting for Sir Cedric Banner to come into the commons. I wanted to see what he would do when he found young Calvert sitting there reading a copy of *Lurid Confessions,* just as bold as life.

Old Sir Cedric came in right at five, on the first bong. He walked over to his chair, swept that high and mighty look around the room, then plopped his bum down. His chair! So his old man used it for fifty years; what does that make Sir Cedric? Well, I won't tell you what it makes him.

He picked up his *Times.* He always gets it unopened and uncut just to be sure that some bloke hasn't been looking at it with his filthy eyes. Then he spread it out to slit the pages. I was afraid he wasn't going to see Calvert. I knew if he ever got into the *Times* he was a goner for an hour. Then old Sir Cedric began to sniff the paper. You'd have thought it was some doll who had just come out of the stage door of the Palladium. But it could have been brandy from the way he acted. Sir Cedric sort of lighted up, like he was pleased with himself because the paper smelled so good.

Then he took a look at Calvert. Honest to God, I think he was getting ready to make old Chris take a whiff of the *Times* for some reason. He was about half-way up out of his chair when he saw what Chris was reading. Hell, Chris might as well have been holding a naked woman on his lap. Sir Cedric went pale and his hands began to tremble; then he got red in the face. I'll bet he went red clear down to his socks. I thought he was going to take a swipe at Calvert, but something kept him from it. It's a good thing it wasn't his father; Old Man Banner would have done it.

Anyhow, Sir Cedric settled back into the chair. He took a few good sniffs of the *Times* and it sort of settled him down. His face went back to its normal counting house tan and his hands quit shaking. He laid the paper aside and got up. The way he stood he looked ten feet tall, and right then I decided I'd never sneak another ten minutes in Sir Cedric's chair. He walked over to Sir Christopher and his finger poked out like a rapier. He wasn't even looking at Chris; he was looking at the magazine.

"I say, Sir Christopher, I do hope you were discreet about bringing that thing in here. The porter is an awful gossip, you know."

Lord, what a voice! If I'd been Chris, I'd have eaten the damned magazine right there on the spot, ruined women and all.

Here again we have the intimacy of the first person, with all of its accompanying advantages and disadvantages. We are running one character—as a living, breathing object—through the interpretation of another character's mind, through the perceptive senses of the narrator's body. To outward appearances this approach might not differ from the first person, subjective, treatment. However, use of the first person, objective, involves a rather specialized story viewpoint which has definite purposes.

For example, let's say our plot demands that we make our character sympathetic but that we must withhold his thoughts and feelings and knowledge from the reader. If we use the third person, objective viewpoint for this character, we cannot get into his mind and we cannot, therefore, get reader sympathy for him. The reader simply wouldn't give a hoot what happened to him. But on the other hand, if we go into his mind subjectively in either the first or third person, we will have to let the story cat out of the bag, and all elements of suspense and/or surprise will evaporate: The story's reason for being will no longer exist. (Remember, we cannot withhold information when it would logically be available to the reader via the mind of the character who is telling the story.)

We can, however, tell our story through another first person who is sympathetic to our character. By means of this viewpoint character's feelings, his reactions, and his sympathy toward the character, the reader will become sympathetic. Then we withhold the requisite information, because it is not logically available to the narrator. His uncertainty resulting from his lack of knowledge can add suspense to the situation.

This approach has also made it possible to tell many

stories which would otherwise be difficult to put across because of most readers' reluctance to identify with an unsavory character. When the undesirable character is revealed objectively by way of a narrator, the reader can identify with the narrator and his problem, whatever it is; he can sit back and watch the activities of a libertine with a clear conscience.

It is also difficult to get reader identification with fictional characters who are permanently disabled. In general, readers just don't like to find themselves playing the role of a blind person, a deaf-mute, or of someone with a deformity or incurable disease. Yet, they may be interested in the dramatic situations which can revolve around such persons. The first person, objective, approach offers a means of telling such a story, since it provides a sufficiently detached viewpoint to allow the reader to feel superior to the unfortunate.

Unless you have more than average skill at spinning words, it is almost a "must" for your first-person narrator to play a definite part in the story, for him to be a sort of a hero, second class. That deadly dull "let me tell you what I saw happen to a fellow last year" business is an old, old hat with a bedraggled feather. It went out of style many, many years ago, along with the stuffy traditions of Sir Cedric's Westchester Club set.

Casual involvement of the narrator by way of introspective philosophical thinking or amazement at the curious ways of human nature is an equally timeworn device. Most editors will no longer accept a story hung upon such a weak peg. It is a part of the historical development of the short story form.

The first person, objective, approach is not a license for the author to dabble in his story. Take the opening of O. Henry's "An Adjustment of Nature" in *The Four Million*:

> In an art exhibition the other day I saw a painting that had been sold for $5,000. The painter was a young scrub out of the West named Kraft, who had a favorite food and a pet theory. His pablum was an unquenchable belief in the Unerring Artistic Adjustment of Nature. His theory was fixed around corned-beef hash with poached egg. There was a story behind the picture, so I went home and let it drip out of a fountain-pen. The idea of Kraft—but that is not the beginning of the story.

Such an opening would hardly be acceptable to modern readers who have been exposed to the results of half a century of improved writing techniques since O. Henry's fountain pen dripped. It is interesting to note that some years ago when a television series was built around a group of O. Henry stories, it was necessary to introduce the author as a participating character. O. Henry's introduction of the story idea and his manipulation of the characters made up the rather obviously contrived plot framework and served as a thread upon which to string the television series.

I believe it is safe to say that considerably more first-person, objective, stories are written than find their way into print. A really good one is a "writer's story"; it is easy to fall in love with this technique, with the freedom of expression and the opportunity it gives the writer to speak, but it is not an easy form to manage.

This viewpoint simply will not work with just any story. It can solve a special problem for the writer in his dealings with a particular plotting problem, but its limitations almost dictate that the need be present before the approach can be successful.

There have been recognized masters of this narrative approach. Damon Runyon immediately comes to mind as one who confined himself almost entirely to this technique. However, strictly speaking, he did not confine himself to the first person, objective viewpoint; he confined himself to plots and characters which fitted the technique he had developed and stamped with his personal imprint. Sir Arthur Conan Doyle revealed Sherlock Holmes through Dr. Watson. This was a solution to a plotting problem: Seen through Holmes' mind, there would have been no mystery. When exposed via Dr. Watson's admiring wonderment, what reader could keep from believing in Holmes' supreme analytical powers?

It is a common error among young writers—young in experience but not necessarily in age—that in the early imitative stage they tend to unfortunate choices when selecting styles of the masters they wish to follow. Most often, the unusual style selected for imitation is like a trademark in its individuality, in its identification with the writer who created it. In many cases, these highly individualistic styles cover or make possible structural faults in writing, plotting, or characterization. When the inexperienced writer attempts the same thing, his treatment more often than not merely magnifies the fault which was masked by the genius of the

creator of the style. The writer becomes "a poor man's
Damon Runyon."

In all cases, when contemplating the first person, objective viewpoint, be certain that your story has a gen-
uine need for this particular technique. If it does not,
the chances are that you will produce an inferior
product. It is usually advisable to experiment with
other viewpoints to see if one of them will do a more
effective job.

Second person, subjective

You go into your club, the Westchester, and you take
your chair, the same chair your father occupied for fifty
years before you. It is a wonderful feeling to know that
it is there waiting for you, a part of the fine old British
tradition which you are helping to maintain. Then you
pick up your uncut copy of the *Times,* look about you,
and realize that the great tradition is dying. You see
nothing but young bounders huddled over slick magazines, unmindful of the years their forebears spent in
this very common room reading of the Empire that they
might mold its policies.

You feel a great regret swelling within you, choking
up into your throat, as you take up your paperknife to
slit your paper. But you cannot help reacting to the
pleasant smell of printer's ink as it wells up out of the
fresh newspaper. You look up and see Sir Christopher
Calvert and decide to let him smell it. Perhaps you can
give him some idea of his responsibilities if you let him
see the proper thing.

You find Sir Christopher's back to you; he is reading
a beastly magazine. You lean forward to get a look at
the title. *Lurid Confessions!* The foulest of trash. You
go hot all over, like being consumed by a great fever,

as you realize the young fool's complete lack of integrity. You know your father would have snatched the magazine from his hands, but such violence is really rather degrading. Christopher wouldn't understand your reason.

You sink back into your chair and let the permeating odor of *Times* ink calm you until you can control your voice. Then you lay the paper aside and walk to Sir Christopher's chair. Gently, but firmly, you tap his shoulder.

"I say, Sir Christopher, I do hope you were discreet about bringing that thing in here. The porter is an awful gossip, you know."

You keep your voice cool and impersonal, hoping to make him realize what a terrible thing he is doing to the dignity of the Empire.

As you can see, this approach makes the going a bit stony. There have been a few good stories written this way, mostly creating a nostalgic I-wish-I-had-been-there feeling in the reader, usually attaining this effect by causing the reader to relive—mentally and emotionally —a portion of his earlier life. It sometimes works in the "letter form" story, which appears rather infrequently these days. But for the most part, so far as fiction is concerned, the "you" approach gets comparatively little extended use. It is awkward to handle, rather dated, and tends to create the impression that the author is intruding upon the reader.

The second-person viewpoint is a useful device to practice until you can control it; then pack it away in your tool chest for future use. When you need it, it will come out naturally, almost unconsciously, and the

chances are that it will serve its purpose smoothly. But
don't strain to reach out and prod your reader with a
you; the result is never happy.

Currently the *you* approach is enjoying something of
a vogue on television and radio programs with a narrator attempting to put the viewers or listeners into
viewpoint: "You are an English knight. Your name is
Sir Cedric Banner. You are a member of the Westchester Club. Other members are destroying the club's traditions by reading slick magazines. Your job: Stop 'em!"
The use of a narrator to attempt to achieve viewer
identification is an old low-grade movie trick which has
not won many accolades in the past from either critics or
viewers.

On paper it does not do nearly as effective a job of
putting the reader into viewpoint as the previously discussed subjective approaches. Certainly it becomes awkward and labored when the writer attempts to sustain it
for any appreciable amount of wordage. So the writer
who is tempted to use this "new" technique as an approach to fictional viewpoint should examine all other
possibilities before becoming involved in its intricacies.
Stories using it are likely to amass a considerable collection of cold, uninitialed rejection slips.

Omniscient viewpoint

In contrast to an entirely objective viewpoint in
which the writer goes into no character's mind but
stands back and views all participants as objects on the
stage before him, the omniscient viewpoint makes the
writer an all-knowing, all-seeing, God-like individual

who can lead the reader into anybody's and everybody's mind at will.

This viewpoint technique may give the writer a feeling of great power and mobility, but personal satisfaction is about the only real benefit he will reap from extended use of it in fiction. I think it can safely be said, certainly so far as fiction is concerned, that this viewpoint is one which is used by writers before they know any better. It was used considerably in Victorian vintage fiction, but fiction writing techniques have come a long way since the quill pen era.

Let us take a short omniscient look at the members of the Westchester Club and see what we get into:

Sir Cedric Banner entered the common room of the Westchester Club to spend the before-dinner half hour reading his London *Times,* occupying the same chair which his father had occupied for fifty years before him. He would seat himself and deliberately slit the pages of his uncut *Times,* as he did every evening at precisely the same hour, knowing all the while that he and he alone was upholding the traditions of the club.

Sir Cedric was acutely aware of the other members, brash young bounders who were deliberately trying to cast aside the old traditions which had meant so much to Britain and to the generation which had bred them. In particular, Sir Cedric abhorred the current fad of reading slick magazines which had taken over among the younger set.

At the very moment Sir Cedric entered the common room, Sir Christopher Calvert was seated in his chair reading a copy of *Lurid Confessions,* making no attempt to hide it from Sir Cedric, even though he knew Sir Cedric's attitude. Sir Christopher felt that Sir Cedric and all like him were stuffy old buzzards who would do well to change, not only change themselves but the policies of Britain before the island tipped and sank under the very weight of their stuffiness.

Watching both Sir Christopher and Sir Cedric, young Lord Handy Mull-Berry didn't give a fig either way. So far as he was concerned, Sir Cedric was stuffy enough, but on the other hand Sir Christopher was a stupid young ass. Lord Handy had inherited his membership in the Westchester Club, along with his title; his principal interest in the club was that it gave him a seat from which to watch the interplay of both factions of British life, providing him with a knowledge of both conservatives and radicals which he could use to pit one against the other.

Had Sir Cedric and Sir Christopher known this, they would probably have laid aside the *Times* and *Lurid Confessions* to join forces against the common enemy. But they didn't.

Sir Cedric had never seen Queen Victoria, but he knew her times. His main mission in life was to bring the English gentleman back up to the stature which he had enjoyed during those golden days when the island was the hub of an empire, before the Americans came with their shiny gadgets and their damnable slick magazines which made everybody want everything whether they could afford it or not.

Lord Handy's mother had been deeply hurt by the Victorian Era. Though the name Mull-Berry allowed her to skirt the edges of the society of English gentlemen and their ladies, her heritage had never permitted her to enter that society. It had left a permanent scar upon her, a scar which had burned to her very heart and which she had somehow managed to imprint upon the heart of her son. He still carried his father's title with his name, but within him he carried his mother's hate of everything that title represented.

That's enough! You could write a hundred pages, and still no reader would be faintly interested in whether Sir Cedric ever got around to clouting Sir Christopher unless he had a phobia regarding confession magazines.

By virtue of the writer's mobility, which is inherent in the omniscient approach, we visited the minds of the three characters who are present and one who is off-stage; we know what makes everybody tick. We know their psychological motivations, why they are as they are. They have no secrets from the reader. Most often, one of two conditions will result: Either you will have a plenitude of sympathy, or you will have no sympathy at all.

For example, in this version of "The Adventures of Sir Cedric," it doesn't appear that we are going to have a single real villain in the yarn. We are going to know why all three members of the Westchester Club are as they are, why they do as they do. This is a ridiculously implausible situation *per se*. In real life such a condition simply never exists. If this state of affairs could be, human strife would be cut to a minimum; most of the people we think are stinkers would turn out to be pretty nice after all, and we could meet them on a middle ground of arbitration. Life would be crystal clear, but it would be dishwater dull. There would be no material from which to make good fiction.

We are back to the point that when you motivate a character's villainy and let the reader into his heart, the reason for the villainy becomes so clear that the reader understands it and sympathizes with the wrong character. Consequently, when the reader returns to the mind of Sir Cedric, he does not find the attitudes and actions of Sir Christopher so terrible unless, by a stroke of luck, we find a reader who identifies with Sir Cedric because of personal beliefs. The story has lost most of its power to engage a large segment of the audience in vicarious emotional participation; it has turned into a series of psychological studies—or something else. Whatever it has become, it is no longer "somebody's story."

Most beginning writers are intrigued by the possibilities inherent in the omniscient viewpoint for analyzing the complicated intertwinings of human relationships. You can show the play of one individual against another, reveal how one person's internal motivations and subconscious feelings cause reactions which rasp against the internal motivations and subconscious feelings of another. It seems like the opportunity to make a real study of human nature from the inside out. And indeed it is an opportunity. The great difficulty is in getting this deep analysis read by more than a handful of intimate acquaintances.

The resulting story has every possibility of turning into a laboratory-like clinical study, a case history rather than a plausible, dramatic, suspenseful story of a living fellowman who feels, thinks, worries, and fears —as we do. Actual case histories are of professional interest to students and practicing scientists, but rarely do these case histories in their raw, undistilled state make good story material. If they did, we would all be out of business and the circulation of the scientific journals would be booming.

But a skilled writer can take the psychologist's case history—a cold Mr. K, or an unlifelike No. 110325—and come up with a dramatic story simply by selecting the right viewpoint. In the great majority of cases the writer does not find necessary control in the omniscient viewpoint.

Let's go back to Sir Cedric and see how the writer loses dramatic impact by using the omniscient approach. When we are in Sir Cedric's mind, we will have no anxiety or terror in anticipation of what Sir Christopher is going to do because we now know how he thinks. He is not a true villain; he is not an unknown quantity.

Indeed, by our narrative approach we have committed ourselves morally to let the reader know if Sir Christopher should have a change of heart which might change his ways. Therefore, pure curiosity as to how the situation is going to turn out is all we have to intrigue the reader. The omniscient viewpoint is, for this reason, an inherently weak method of narration for arousing vicarious participation by the reader. The greatest drawback is probably a matter of its sheer implausibility, because it robs the reader of that curiosity which we experience in normal human relationships: "What is John going to do?" "What will Mary do when she finds out?"

Under the conditions of the omniscient approach, a reader is not living through a story with one participating character; he is somewhere above looking down upon and into all. As a result of so much familiarity, he is likely to feel contempt for each. Sir Cedric will seem stupid for worrying about Sir Christopher's magazine reading; Sir Christopher will seem stupid for paying attention to Sir Cedric's stuffy attitude.

There is one variety of story which almost demands the omniscient viewpoint. This is the story in which all of the principal characters—usually not more than two—are sympathetic to the reader but at odds with each other. Reader reaction is obtained by arousing within the reader a suspenseful desire for these characters to patch up their differences and get together. It is not a particularly easy story to tell effectively, and it is seldom a story of great emotional depth.

So you will do well to look at your plot long and hard before you decide to commit yourself to use of the omniscient viewpoint.

There is another occasional but handy use for the omniscient viewpoint in fiction which usually comes up early in the story when you want to set the stage for the dramatic situation. For maximum effect, or, more accurately, minimum interruption of the reader's sympathies, this had better take place in the beginning, in the narrative hook, before you involve the reader with a character.

At this stage of a story, it is often possible to go into the minds of several story characters as a way of depicting the setting in which your principal character is going to act. Then, after setting the stage, so to speak, with the people in the environment of your viewpoint character, you make a transition into the third person, subjective, to tell the story through that character. In this way it is often possible to intrigue the reader into wanting to read about someone placed in such a situation.

It is also possible to get information across to the reader more quickly with less wordage than would be possible through the viewpoint of your leading character. In addition, you can put across information which would be impossible to communicate to the reader from the viewpoint of your leading character.

But beware that you do not become so intent upon the writer's problem of setting up the situation and planting information that you completely disregard the reader or fail to involve him in your character's problem or emotional situation. No matter how fine a story you may have written, if the reader does not get through the opening to read it, you have wasted your effort.

Using the omniscient viewpoint in the story opening can also provide a means of planting a fact, a feature, a character, or an event which (because of the limitations of the plot and the viewpoint) would otherwise have to be introduced so late that it would seem contrived. If the hurricane, the talking parrot, or the taxi driver who doesn't know his way about the city enters the story on page sixteen of an eighteen-page manuscript, it will appear to have been dragged in at the writer's convenience rather than to have occurred naturally.

in the story. However, if it has been planted in the narrative hook story opening, it forecasts an event to come—whether so stated or not—and the writer will not be accused of thinking it up out of the blue to make his story come out right in the end.

And so you have viewpoint: the writer's most difficult problem and his greatest tool. Many writers use this tool unconsciously without realizing what they are doing. Not infrequently, as I know from personal experience and knowledge gained, unfortunately after the fact, one story will be successful because the viewpoint is correct and consistent throughout the yarn, building up vicarious participation on the part of the reader. The next story can bounce from market to market, accumulating a collection of rejection slips because the viewpoint is either not the one best adapted to the particular story or because it is not the one which will produce the greatest impact upon the particular group of readers to whom the story will naturally appeal. Or perhaps the difficulty will be that the viewpoint is confused, more often than not a combination of several approaches, resulting in a diffusion of emotional impact rather than a concerted attack upon the reader's feelings.

There is another old saying: "The writer must be in viewpoint if his story isn't." The writer must feel the message of his story; he must want to tell it. This feeling must be an intense feeling about a certain sympathetic approach. In other words, if he does not write strictly "in viewpoint" with his character, he must personally be "in sympathy" with his character.

For example, I might be in sympathy with Sir Cedric, I might be in sympathy with Sir Christopher, or I might be in sympathy with Lord Mull-Berry. It must be one; it can't be all. I cannot feel for all three in the same story and expect the story to have any great effect upon the reader. In my viewpoint treatment of a particular character in my story, I might find it necessary to shift to the viewpoint of another character, but I can never be sympathetically attached to a viewpoint which does not reflect my feeling and sympathy for the goal of my viewpoint character. The result will be fatal to the story. If you find that you cannot concentrate your sympathies into a single character's viewpoint, you will spend your time much more wisely if you drop the whole idea into the wastebasket and do something else.

Unfortunately, viewpoint technique does not come in a do-it-yourself kit, complete with glue and directions for assembly; at least I could not find it. In fact, I did not want to find it. In the early stages, as is the case with most students of writing, I refused to admit the necessity for such techniques; I had heard about them, but it was obvious that such details would get in the way of one's creative imagination—I thought.

So I wrote by ear—by the yard. It was a beneficial exercise, even if it was unremunerative. The thought of producing ten pages of manuscript, twenty pages, or even a hundred pages began to hold no terrors. Words flowed freely from my typewriter. Eventually it began to seep through the stone wall of my creative ideals that something must be wrong with a great many of those words.

Motivated by the unfriendly sterility of one printed rejection slip after another, I began to assimilate information from practice, experimentation, and re-writing. I filled to overflowing many wastebaskets with crumpled pages. Eventually I discovered that technique is a servant to one's creative ideals rather than an obstacle before them.

More recently, in working with other writers, I have discovered that viewpoint can be explained rather easily, but no amount of explanation can make it work for a writer unless he is willing to practice with it.

Inevitably, if the writer has never before attempted to manipulate viewpoint, his initial results are stiff and awkward, self-conscious, and disappointing. However, one gains facility by practice. *You simply cannot learn to write without writing.* A half a million words—new, freshly written words—is not an unreasonable amount of practice.

The following chapters detail the techniques involved in implementing the various facets of *viewpoint*. I learned these techniques—even after being told about them by others—only by practice upon my own material and by editing the works of other writers and students.

Eventually the handling of viewpoint becomes virtually automatic. It becomes a part of the writer, something he does without conscious effort, just as we learn to commit our thoughts to paper without awareness of the pen, the typewriter, or the microphone into which we are dictating.

Viewpoint becomes simply a tool at the writer's fingertips. However, no matter how much you practice, from time to time you—like most writers—will find yourself making stupid mistakes. You will discover these mistakes after you have received your favorite story back from your favorite editor, the one you wanted to impress more than anyone else. Vigilance must be eternal.

If you have never played with the idea of viewpoint and its ramifications, I believe you will profit greatly from finding yourself a Sir Cedric and approaching him from every possible type of viewpoint for practice. Although your Sir Cedric may end up in the wastebasket, along with his *Times* and Sir Christopher's *Lurid Confessions,* you will learn a lot from him on how to control your reader's sympathies and emotions by way of the cold black and white of the printed page.

IV

LETTING PEOPLE INTERVENE

———•◆•———

The characters are the most important elements of any fictional or, for that matter, real-life drama. The actors form the link between the events and the beholder, whether he be a reader or a viewer, whether the medium be the printed page or one of the performing arts. As Michener put it when he was setting the scene in his introduction to *Tales of the South Pacific,* "But whenever I start to talk about the South Pacific, people intervene."

The fiction reader reads for entertainment, and the majority of readers of fiction are entertained in direct proportion to their involvement with one or more participating characters. The final test of a fiction writer is most certainly his ability to portray character. We remember the well-portrayed character long after we have forgotten his creator's name. Some characters are so graphically drawn that their names find their way into our dictionaries because the mere mention of the fictional character does a better job of delineating a segment of society than anything else we could possibly say: Shylock, Hawkshaw, Pickwick, Uncle Tom, Babbitt, Milquetoast, and many others.

The fiction reading audience can be divided into four groups, depending on the reasons for their involvement or identification with invented characters:

Vicarious participants: Those who enjoy the drama because they can identify and/or sympathize with one or more of the characters or because they enjoy experiencing the emotions undergone by the characters. (As Alfred Hitchcock has said, "Some phases of fear we enjoy. Or I would not be in business.")

Superior beings: Those who like to read about someone less fortunate because they enjoy feeling superior. (Though this may not be recognized, or admitted, by individual readers, it is a psychological reality of one of the reasons for reading.)

Play watchers: Those who frankly enjoy, either emotionally or intellectually, the entertainment which is being provided by the participating characters. (Many of these readers are capable of enjoying a story even though they may not believe in or accept the theme or message.)

The curious: Those who, upon adequate exposure to a character, will read on to find out how he is going to come out in his involvement in a situation. (Many of these readers are comparatively nondiscriminating in their tastes and are likely to say they "read to pass the time.")

By far the largest number of the total reading audience is included in the first group. This group probably makes up most of the so-called "mass audience." From the best I have been able to determine by research, the second and third groups bulk approximately equal and the fourth group is the smallest. Obviously, depending upon the writer's skill in characterization— or perhaps his feeling for his character—a given piece may "cross lines" to appeal to more than one or perhaps all of the four audience groups. Then the story is likely to be cited critically as having that rather vague quality called "universality." *

For example, Elwood P. Dowd, the leading character in Mary Chase's Pulizer Prize-winning play, *Harvey,* is an alcoholic—not a likely character to attract a mass audience on the basis of simple vicarious identification. However, the play and its subsequent motion picture version did have mass audience appeal for reasons which encompass substantial portions of all four of these audience groups.

Elwood P. Dowd appeals to the *vicarious participants* because the story, as presented from his viewpoint, projects a character so human and warm that the vicarious participants, alcoholics or not, can understand the mo-

* Critically, *universality* has been so variously used that one needs to identify its meaning. For example, one definition has it that in order to achieve universality the symbolistic implications must have religious significance, like the reviewer who said *The Old Man and the Sea* is a morality play in which the fisherman is punished by having his fish destroyed because he made promises for offerings and penance which he never intended to fulfill. And it is sometimes used synonymously with mass audience appeal. Here I am using *universality* to refer to those qualities of character which are common to mankind.

tivation behind his being what he is and can sympathize with him when self-seeking relatives attempt to have him committed to a sanitarium.

What better character is there than an alcoholic to provide the *superior beings,* temperate or otherwise, with a feeling of well-being? They may criticize the message or the ending, but above all they can be smugly happy that there is no chance of their becoming involved in such a plight.

Harvey has superbly developed characterization, good scenes, and good gimmicks. The philosophy or message is revealed through the characters as a development and projection of their personalities, and the *play watcher* does not feel that he is sitting in front of a pulpit. He can relax and truly say that the characters are providing him with entertainment which appeals both to his emotional and intellectual being.

The curious find sufficient suspense and novelty in the situation to satisfy their interests. There is the leading character's reaction to the attempts to get him committed to an institution, revealing a different side of his personality. Then there is the separate factor of a large, invisible rabbit which only the leading character can see. All of this combines into enough what-will-happen-to-him-next? and what's-he-going-to-do-now? to keep the curious spectators through the last act.

In addition, there is a bit of Everyman in Elwood P. Dowd which expresses itself in defiance of accepted social convention. There is not a spectator in the audience who would not like to emulate him when he replies to the ubiquitous social taradiddle "You must come over sometime" by asking "When?" And when Dowd whips out his datebook to toll off the nights he has free— *If only I had just thought of that and dared to do it!* Every member of the audience can project himself into such a scene as he is remembering lost opportunities.

It is important for the writer to note that while the play has appeal on various audience levels, the appeal to each level is a separate entity because it is based upon a different motivation; the viewpoint character approaches each audience level from a different angle.

I used a play to illustrate this particular point because it is frequently helpful for the prose writer to look upon his characters as actors. The prose writer has one big disadvantage in comparison to the dramatist: There are no living actors on his stage to project the personalities he creates. The prose writer must bring his paper people to life and show them to his reader. Viewpoint is the tool by which this is achieved.

The prose writer's one big advantage over the dramatist is viewpoint: He can take his readers into his character's mind without having to depend upon soliloquies, songs, and other contrived devices which can often strain the observer's credulity. The prose writer must realize this advantage and capitalize on it to the fullest.

Showing vs. telling

The distinction between showing and telling is vital to the writer's story, whether the character is being treated "in viewpoint" or objectively. Let's say that the writer is doing a story called "Pamela's Rebellion" concerning a young housewife who revolted because of having to iron her husband's shirts, something that many a housewife could readily understand.

Naturally, the seed for such a story might have been planted at the ironing board; and just as naturally, the writer might get to her typewriter for the big decision of the story just after finishing a laundry basket of ironing—while she is in the mood. She might write something like this:

> Pamela ironed the last cuff of the last white shirt of a full two-a-day week's worth of shirts and collapsed on the bed to regain the strength that had drained from her perspiring body. But she could not close her eyes. There in front of her, dangling from the top of the clothes hamper, was the beginning of next week's wash, where Jim had thrown his dirty shirt during the scramble to change his clothes to go out to dinner. It wasn't bad enough that he had to entertain clients every night; she had to stay at home and iron the shirts for him to wear while he was doing it. Pamela felt the anger building within her.

To the writer who had just finished an ironing, that paragraph connoted all of the boredom and drudgery of the tedious household chore: Weary shoulders, aching back, parboiled fingers, ankles swollen from standing at the ironing board. Then to see another dirty shirt! Who wouldn't rebel? . . . And the writer was incredulous at an editorial criticism which said, "It seems to us that Pamela's revolt is not sufficiently motivated."

Certainly the paragraph is in viewpoint, otherwise the reader could not know that Pamela is bitterly lamenting the fact that Jim is out living it up with clients while she stays home to iron. This complaint is motivated by the drudgery of ironing. But is enough of that drudgery communicated to the reader to make Pamela's reaction plausible?

The reader is told that Pamela collapsed on the bed after she finished her ironing because she was weak from perspiring. That is all. The writer did not let the reader feel the tired shoulders, aching back, swollen ankles, burned fingers, or a single rivulet of perspiration. She merely *told* the reader about Pamela's state without showing any of the details that caused it—details with which the reader might identify as a result of personal experience at the ironing board.

Dramatic decisions—leading to rebellions or whatever—are based upon emotional experiences. It is not enough for the writer to tell how Pamela felt as a result of the experience; the writer must show the experience building up. Then an act or a decision stemming from that experience will be motivated with sufficient strength to be plausible, because the reader will have vicariously lived through the motivation.

Emotional states and the physical feelings attendant to them are universal; they are experienced by people. They cannot be communicated to people in a wordy vacuum of telling, and the writer cannot allow them to be experienced by his character while he is offstage.

Anger is a violent emotion and lends itself readily

to examination because evidences of it are usually forth-right if not crude. The chemistry is the same in Pamela as it is in an Australian aborigine: There is motivation, the pang of recognition of danger or an object of hate, then an excessive secretion of adrenalin which gives extra energy, either to run away or to fight. This is the clinical side of what was going on when "Pamela felt the anger building within her." But how did she feel?

The writer must examine himself in the emotional state into which he is projecting his character. To show the heat of anger, you must feel the heat of anger. How do you feel when you are angry? Does your belly go tight? Is there a sinking sensation in your stomach? Do your insides seem to creep and crawl? Does your mouth feel dry? Do tears seep uncontrollably from your eyes? Can you feel the blood leave your face and the muscles around your eyes and mouth grow so tight that they feel numb? Do your legs shake with tension? Do your lips tremble so that you cannot talk?

What do you do when you are angry? Are you noisy? Do you stamp your feet or curse or shout? Does your voice change pitch and quality? Do you speak hoarsely or quietly? Do you throw things? Do your hands clench until the fingers hurt and cramp? Do you stand stiffly frozen, no matter what you want to do? Or do you fling yourself about in an aimless fury?

Most of these reactions are common to everyone—easily recognizable; but the selection of details to show anger depends upon the personality of the character you are building and the emotional tone of your story.

To a certain extent, the narrative style is determined by the type of story you are writing, but the basic techniques of *showing* are the same in any case.

You do not want to make the mistake of telling your reader, "Anger makes me want to hit things." Your reader cannot experience this. Instead, show the reader your hands balling up into fists until they hurt. Show your body becoming taut and ready to explode as the heat of the motivation boils up in you. Then, when you find yourself senselessly pounding a table or a wall or an opponent, the reader will know why it happened because he has been there. He will have experienced feelings and actions which he has in common with the viewpoint character. After the writer has expressed the heat of anger on paper in the person of his viewpoint character, he will not have to tell the reader that "Pamela felt the anger building within her."

Now let's look at one of the most common examples of ineffective writing on the objective side of showing vs. telling:

> Pamela saw Jim as she entered the bedroom. It was obvious from his distraught face and frantic actions that he already knew there were no clean shirts.

The actor is on stage, but the writer is showing neither his appearance nor his actions. There is absolutely nothing here for the reader to see. What is it about Jim's face that communicates his distraught emotional state? Is it alternately turning red and blue? Are his eyes rolling in his head? Is he foaming at the mouth? Are the wrinkles in his forehead rolling and breaking like surf on the beach? If you show the selected, *specific details* which communicate the emotional state, you won't have to tell the reader something "was obvious"; it will become obvious to the reader as he sees it. You won't even have to put a tag to your Jim's emotional state.

The phrase, "frantic actions", shows nothing. What is Jim doing that reveals his frantic state? Is he lighting one cigarette after another and leaving them burning in a ring about the ash tray? Is he trying to straighten out a crumpled shirt? Is he cleaning spots off one with lighter fluid and waving it in the air to get the smell out? Make it a rule never to tell your character's emotional state by an abstract description of his actions. Show the actions which reveal it.

This technique of showing was not developed yesterday. Look at the opening of O. Henry's "The Gift of the Magi":

One dollar and eighty-seven cents. That was all. And sixty cents of it was in pennies. Pennies saved one and two at a time by bulldozing the grocer and the vegetable man and the butcher until one's cheeks burned with the silent imputation of parsimony that such close dealing implied. Three times Della counted it. One dollar and eighty-seven cents. And the next day would be Christmas.

At the end of that 67-word opening the reader knows Della's problem; he knows with his heart and his mind that her financial condition is desperate. He has seen her count and recount an insignificant odd sum of small change—a universal act that everyone has done at one time or another. He has been told the motivating fact of how she acquired it, a penny or two at a time, by the painful process of haggling; her resulting embarrassment has been shown by a selected, specific physical reaction which is common to all readers.

The secret of doing this successfully is to project yourself into the viewpoint character to find out how he feels, and then show those feelings to the reader. To portray your objectively viewed characters, see them in your mind's eye as the viewpoint character does and show the reader what you see.

"Pamela's Rebellion" was an early, unsuccessful story by one of my students. Later the author sent me a copy of her first check—for another story: "I finally got the idea," she wrote. "I discovered that in my mind's eye—that you used to insist I had—I am really seeing every character I write about portrayed by some movie actor I have seen. I show what he is doing, and you can see the results."

Take the reader with your character

Sir Walter Scott once wrote, "There is no heroic poem in the world but is at bottom a biography, the life of a man." The fiction writer must never relax from the truth of that statement. Every dramatic story is basically a segment of the life of one of the story characters. The reader must be allowed to participate with the character throughout that segment of his life.

Every writer is plagued by a tendency to tell about the situation in which his character is involved and then plop the reader into the middle of the resulting emotional conflict. Let's look at an example of how it can happen:

The two policemen, one in uniform and the other in plain clothes, grabbed the redheaded holdup man and roughly dragged him out of the Coach and Eight. A small, silvery cap pistol dangled from the limp fingers of one hand. The man in uniform took the pistol, and the crowd which was beginning to accumulate pressed closer. [*Up to this point the reader is not in viewpoint. We are simply looking at the event, getting pure action and facts, from outside the viewpoint character.*]

Red looked into their faces and saw contempt and accusation. [*Here we go into Red's viewpoint to learn what he saw.*] He had to make them understand. [*And what he thought.*]

"It was for little Tommy," he told a baldheaded man with a tiny black mustache. "I've got to get a dollar to—"

But they hustled him away before he could finish. The policeman was behind him, twisting his arm until it went numb. The man in street clothes walked close beside him.

"All I wanted was a dollar so Tommy can buy his mother a birthday present." The plainclothesman wouldn't even look at him. "Look, mister, what would you do if you found your son trying to steal perfume for his mother?"

The policeman behind him made a snorting sound.

"All I wanted was a dollar. I was going to bring it back tomorrow, just as soon as Mrs. Watson gets home and pays me for taking care of her dog."

Basically, the difficulty here is caused by the writer's not having taken the reader along with the viewpoint character from the beginning of the story, during that period when Red was making the decision which got him into trouble. Red's holdup was motivated by a basic human desire, as we begin to discover after the fact, but the impact is greatly weakened by the reader's absence when the motivation created itself in the character.

We might have started like this, in Red's mind from the first sentence:

When Red found little Tommy in the drugstore trying to snitch a bottle of perfume, he knew that it was a darned good thing he had decided to come and see him, even if it wasn't his regular visiting day. Luckily, Red got the perfume out of Tommy's pocket and back onto the counter while the proprietor was still busy with a customer at the prescription counter.

"Now let's go over to the park and talk about this."

"But, Daddy, I just got to get some 'fume for Mummy. Tomorrow's her birthday."

Red had forgotten that tomorrow was Irene's birthday, not that she would be looking for any presents from him. He hustled Tommy outside.

"That would be stealing, Tommy. You must never steal."

Tommy drew the bright silver cap pistol from the holster at his belt and ran across the park to give a passing squirrel a quick "bang-bang."

"Got him!"

Red caught up with him. "Did you hear me, Tommy?"

"Daddy, can I have my 'lowance today insteada Saturday?"

"Sure, but—I—I—I didn't bring it with me, Tommy."

Another squirrel got a "bang-bang."

"You s'pose the man in the store will give me a bottle of 'fume for my gun?"

That hurt. Red had given him the cap pistol for the Fourth of July. He took it from Tommy and ran his fingers over the silvery metal. The butt cupped snugly into his hand. It was very light, but it looked very real.

"I doubt it, son. But I'll tell you what I'll do. I'll get your allowance and meet you right here at four-thirty. That will be a half an hour before your mother gets home from work. Then you can go over to the store and buy the perfume for her."

Red held out the pistol to Tommy.

"You keep it, Daddy, 'til Saturday when you're s'posed to come and bring my 'lowance. You can keep my gun like the man keeps your watch 'til you bring him back his money."

Automatically Red rubbed his empty wrist. "Yeah, sure." He slipped the cap pistol into his overcoat pocket. "Four-thirty," he said and hurried off across the park.

By four o'clock Red knew that he wasn't going to have the dollar. Nobody wanted a yard cut in November. All the leaves had been raked. There was no snow to shovel, and Mrs. Watson wouldn't be home until tomorrow to pay him for taking care of her dog. The cleaner with the MAN WANTED sign in the window didn't want him until Monday. The man in the little cage in Joe's Used Clothing laughed in his face.

"A dollar for *that* coat! I'll sell you a better one for four bits."

The clock in the tower of St. Alban's was tolling four as Red came in front of the Coach and Eight. He had worked there until they bought a dishwashing machine. He shoved his hands into his overcoat pockets and found Tommy's pistol.

Now it has taken us longer to get to the restaurant, but the reader has lived through the situation with the leading character right from the beginning of that segment of his life. He has dramatic insight into the story because he has been with Red as the situation developed. The reader may not think Red should hold up a restaurant for a dollar, but he will understand much better why he is doing it than if he first met Red as he was being hustled down the street by a pair of policemen. The reader has not been left out of the story at the critical point.

This same difficulty of leaving the reader out of the story frequently occurs when the writer becomes so intent upon setting up the conditions necessary to the situation that he forgets to take the reader with his character. Instead of letting the reader get to know the character as the character develops, the writer develops the character for his reader. The result might go something like this:

> Since his divorce, Red Bauslin's life had been a continuous round of odd jobs. He had kicked the bottle that had caused the trouble, but nobody would believe it—least of all Irene. The obvious answer was to go someplace else, where he wasn't known. But that would mean giving up his one-time-a-week with Tommy, so Red continued to run errands, walk dogs, cut grass, shovel snow, or anything else he could find to do to scrape up a spare dollar to give to little Tommy every Saturday.
>
> One Tuesday morning in November, Red went past the park over by Irene's apartment house on the off

chance that he might find Tommy playing there. Instead, he found him in the drugstore across the street trying to steal a bottle of perfume to give to Irene for her birthday. It became obvious to Red that somehow he had to get his hands on a dollar so he could give Tommy his allowance in advance.

It is the same old trouble: All telling and no showing makes a good yarn a dull tale as the writer hastens along to get Red to the big scene which is really going to put him into hot water. The reader is given only facts and, consequently, can absorb them only with his mind. The story has no heart.

This approach is founded on a basic misconception of the origin of a story. This story or any other which might lay claim to dramatic force happens not because of the facts but because of a character who is reacting to those facts. Red was getting into trouble because of his heart. Dramatic insight into the story can be communicated to the reader only by showing the reader Red's inner soul.

Another common version of this difficulty is likely to occur when the writer decides to start off with a big bang—in other words, with the leading character right smack in the middle of an emotional high point. The resulting opening is usually something like this:

Martha Treece looked up from her book and squarely into the big round blue muzzle of a gun. Behind the gun was a pair of beady black eyes. Every fiber of Martha's body tingled, and a great choking hurt came into her throat as she tried to scream.

Martha may be scared silly, but the reader is going to start yawning—if he doesn't turn on to something else—because the reader hasn't the foggiest notion of who Martha is, where she is, what she is doing, or who the beady-eyed gunman might be. Let's see what this might have meant to the writer:

Martha Treece turned on the radio and curled up in the big chair for another night of waiting for Henry. She knew that somebody had to go when people got sick, but it seemed that it always had to be Henry.

Martha picked up her book from the coffee table. *Night of Terror.* She smiled at the picture of the screaming woman on the book jacket. Thank heaven for mystery stories! She opened the book and started to read.

"In spite of Detective Fry's not believing her, Carmen was sure after overhearing the telephone conversation that she was next. 'She knows too much,' the grating voice had said. So she decided to hide behind the drapes in her room, instead of going to bed. . . ."

Martha heard the distant wail of a screaming siren and looked up at the clock. Only eight-thirty. What if it were an accident? And what if Henry had to— She turned the radio louder and went back to the book to keep from thinking about it.

"Carmen felt the dusty drapes tickling her nose as the French windows opened. All she could see through the tiny slit was a shadow, but that shadow was enough. It was a hand, holding a gun. If she—"

The music stopped abruptly.

"We interrupt this program to bring you a bulletin. The Penrock Supermarket has been held up at gun-point . . ."

Martha felt the pain of her teeth catching her lower lip. Penrock was only two blocks away.

". . . identified from photographs as Joseph Mc-Querry, alias Mack Joseph, one of the ten most wanted men, the bandit was last seen on foot, carrying a brown paper bag. He is armed and dangerous. He—"

Martha switched off the radio and listened to the creaking whisper of the empty house. Now she wished she would hear another siren. At least she would know the police were around. The front door! A mist of perspiration gathered on her forehead. Had the front door squeaked? But she had locked it. She loosened her grip on the book and smoothed the crumpled page.

"Carmen felt the dusty drapes tickling her nose as the French windows opened. All—"

A thousand prickles ran across Martha's scalp as she heard a man clear his throat. Then there was the whispering silence again, and all she could hear was the blood pumping in her temples. She picked out the plink of the leaky kitchen faucet and realized that what she had heard must have been water gurgling down the drain. She wiped her palm down the leg of her slacks and winced from her digging fingernails. She forced her eyes back to the book.

"Carmen felt the dusty drapes—"

Then Martha heard the crackling of paper. *A brown paper bag!* She looked up, squarely into the big round blue muzzle of a gun.

If the reader is a woman with an active imagination and has ever spent a night alone in a house, she is jolly well right along with Martha in the middle of her emotional state because she was with her when the situation was building. Some of her own past experiences have been brought back to her. She has identified with fear of a lonely, too-silent house when the tiniest sound becomes magnified by terror.

Regardless of the situation and the character and the emotional level or tone of the story, the writer will obtain maximum impact by using viewpoint to take his reader with his character during that all-important segment of the story when the situation is building up around the character. Unless the reader is present, reader identification is virtually impossible.

A story attains dramatic significance in the telling almost in direct proportion to the extent that "people intervene" between the writer and his subject matter. The writer who starts to write about the early development of the West, for example, and finds he is projecting himself into the very soul of a person involved in his account can come up with a living story. The writer who does not find a person evolving from his material is likely to produce only an accumulation of facts and information. The most effective of the writers who deal with factual material—whether they are writing fiction or fact—allow the real people of their material to intervene, thus producing stories which burn with dramatic fire. In reality, the dividing line between fiction and fact is invisible because it is so often hidden behind the techniques of viewpoint.

Presenting your character

The gulf which appears to exist between various levels of published material might seem to preclude telling your story to a particular audience. However, this barrier is more often a product of the writer's mind than an actuality of the craft of fiction. The difference between the opposite ends of the span of literature has nothing to do with what story can be told; the point is how to tell the story. The difference is really in the method of handling the viewpoint of your story.

To demonstrate this, let's contrast the same scene as it might be written for a confessions audience and for the readers of a women's magazine. First the confessions version:

> I looked out at the gray sky and even through the window could feel the stinging air permeating my body. It had to be more in my mind than in my body, and then I realized that the coldness was really in my heart—the coldness of fear, because today I must do something about having two husbands. I was going to be face-to-face with them, both at the same time.
>
> On one side would be Rupert, oldish with rheumatism, bitter and vindictive, not at Henry but at me, because I had left him in his time of need. Regret touched at my heart because I had liked Rupert so much. But the thought of Henry was enough to push any such thoughts away.
>
> Henry was so young that his anger came to a boil almost without notice. The cold inside my body grew colder, seeming to reach clear down to my toes. Henry might kill me, and Rupert would actually help him. Fear caught in my throat and I could not breathe.

Here the facts of the situation come from outside of the character's body and are transformed into positive physical, mental, and emotional reactions. In effect, the writer has done the reader's thinking and feeling for her by way of the viewpoint character.

Now let's see how it might be done in one of the women's magazines:

Janet watched the naked branches of the oak fretted against the leaden sky, moving stiffly in the cold, whining wind. The oak was little, like Rupert—old and a bit rheumatic. And the wind was like Henry, vigorously youthful, sweeping along without regard for what might be in its path. There was much she liked about Rupert, even yet. True, he was crotchety, but that gave him individuality and unexpected spunk at times. Yes, he would have spunk.

He was not one to put up with any foolishness, even from a man of Henry's violent temper. The oak careened and snapped back as if striking at the wind. . . . Or any foolishness from Janet. She bit her lip and had to look away from the window. Rupert was a great one to get at the cause of any trouble, and she was the cause of all of his—and Henry's. And if there was ever a man of direct action, it was Henry.

No longer could she put off doing something about the fact that she was married to both of them. Janet shivered and looked out the window again. It would be as if she were out there between the wind and the oak, being blown against the tree, seared on one side with cold and gouged on the other by flaying, wind-blown branches.

Here the viewpoint character is not experiencing the situation in the same way as the confessions character. Instead of the situation being transformed into physical and emotional reactions within the viewpoint character, the viewpoint character sees the world as a set of symbols representing the elements of her situation. In this way, the reader is given freedom of imagination to interpret the viewpoint character's picture of the world into physical and, particularly, emotional reactions.

Carried considerably further, this is precisely the method of a symbol-charged "quality" or "literary" version:

Janet was awakened by the empty bed beside her, cold to the reach of her hand and foot. She drew back into the warmth her body had created. She felt like the piece in a jigsaw puzzle next to the vacant space created by one that was lost. Yes, damn it! That's what life was, a jigsaw puzzle. You had to have every piece or the thing wouldn't hang together.

She sat up in bed and looked at the two pictures on her dressing table. Today she would put her life back together. She gathered the bedclothes about her, but the cold was coming from inside of her rather than from outside. Her trouble was not a missing piece; she had too many pieces for her jigsaw puzzle. She would have to do something about having two husbands, and it would mean being face-to-face with them —both at the same time.

Rupert, oldish with rheumatism, would be bitter because she had left him in his time of need. Rupert would hardly fill the vacant space, but he wouldn't give up his place in the puzzle, that she knew. And Henry? Young and angry, sweeping along without regard for what might be in his path, Henry would fill the void and to spare. Janet frowned. Henry would push all the other pieces out of place.

Janet watched her hand, inexorably moving toward the telephone beside the bed. She could not stop it, even as she felt the crushing pain of being caught between two pieces of her life that were trying to squeeze in where there was space for only one.

Here we have the same story, but the entire viewpoint has been directed toward the single idea that life is a jigsaw puzzle and the individual spends it trying to find enough pieces or to make the pieces fit. The accent is on idea rather than on emotional impact. However, the viewpoint furnishes the vehicle by which the symbolism is communicated to the reader. If it were not for Janet's reactions, from within her viewpoint, the story would be little more than a philosophical essay. In such a story, the symbolism may or may not be as obvious as it is in the above example. The depth and nature of the symbolism is a matter of viewpoint. If the viewpoint character is incapable of interpreting the situation, the meaning can be left to the reader.

The above three versions are written in apparently different styles for obviously different types of publications. Each would probably attract a different reading audience. The difference from one to the next is not a change in the story's plot line; the manner of narration is not markedly different. The basic difference comes from the depth and manner of penetrating the character's viewpoint.

In the first example, viewpoint is used as a vehicle by which to furnish the reader with the character's thoughts, physical feelings, and emotional reactions so thoroughly that there can be no misinterpretation. In the second version, the viewpoint character sees and feels the world about her as a changing pattern of imagery from which the reader can interpret feelings and emotional reactions with little difficulty. In the third version, the character is the focal point of an idea which the writer is transmitting to the reader by way of the character's intellectual reaction to the situation.

The writer must keep his approach to his character consistent within a given story. A mixture of the above three levels in the same story would create a fuzzy, confused effect which would probably not hold the attention of any of the three audiences.

Basically the discussion in this chapter has been concerned with certain viewpoint techniques which particularly enhance the writer's portrayal of the intervention of people. The dramatic insight which provides the viewpoint must come from within the writer as a feeling for his materials; this is the part of himself which every fiction writer must put into everything he writes.

Every writer must at least once suffer the experience of trying to write a story which he does not feel. It usually happens when some well-meaning friend shows up with an idea "that you've just *got* to write." The situation seems dramatic, and the plot line looks good. . . . But after innumerable false starts and frustrating pages, the writer learns that he cannot write somebody else's story: The people refuse to intervene, and the narrative lies upon the page as shallow as the ink with which it is written.

Look for the story in which you can feel a living viewpoint.

V

USING VIEWPOINT
AS A YARDSTICK

———•—•———

Students of fiction writing are perpetually seeking quantitative answers and positive, unchanging rules, perhaps because editorial requirements are normally prescribed by word-lengths, or columns, or pages, or areas of white space to be filled: "How much description of my characters should I have?" "Should I start out with my hero's full name?" and many more.

The answers to such questions can never be quantitative or positive, because writing fiction is a creative process which must beat with the individual writer's pulse, uninhibited by the strangulation of coldly calculated rules. Any art which can be codified is no longer art. Fortunately, however, viewpoint does provide the writer with guidelines by which he can determine whether he has too much or too little in certain areas and whether he has done right or wrong in others.

This chapter will discuss character background, description, and naming—the three areas in which positive answers are most frequently sought.

How much of the character's life?

The discussion of a story as a segment of the main character's life inevitably brings up the question of how much of your character's life to show. The answer is as variable as the reply to the old conundrum, "How long is a piece of string?"

In earlier times, particularly in the case of a novel, it was generally considered *de rigueur* for the writer to begin his story with the birth of the hero, if not with a thorough rundown on his ancestral background, with such section subtitles as "Concerning as Much of the Birth of the Foundling as Is Necessary or Proper to Acquaint the Reader with the Beginning of This History" (Henry Fielding's *Tom Jones*). In part the change has come about because of the development of more effective techniques, but in a larger part because readers in today's world are not particularly preoccupied with or dependent upon ancestral heritages and social backgrounds. In these times, reader identification with such an approach would be at a low level.

Of course, this is not to say that a character's background should never, never be portrayed. If a particular story is created by the nature of a character who is so thoroughly a product of his background that the background makes the character, then enough of that character's background needs to be shown to provide motivation for the character.

Sometimes this may be accomplished, particularly

early in the story, by a quick objective narrative sketch which can characterize at the same time it is establishing time, place, and social atmosphere. Such a beginning can be objective up to a point: The actual motivating scene, event, action, or whatever can be shown most effectively from inside the viewpoint character. Motivation is an obligatory part of that segment of the principal character's life which creates the drama. The following story opening uses the narrative sketch technique:

Sergeant Paul McAdams was a product of the frontier. Born in Kentucky in 1844, he had been barely five when his father quit the misery of following a plow for the perils of following a rumor of gold westward toward California. Paul was the sole survivor of their wagon.

The Conestoga had been too heavy to keep pace with the lighter prairie schooners. A lone Comanche brave marked it like a hungry wolf stalking a sore-footed steer, and a stabbing lance tore Angus McAdams away from the wagon seat and away from his dream of gold.

Paul's earliest and most abiding memory was of seeing his mother scalped as she ran from the wagon to decoy the Comanche warrior away from him. It was small wonder that Paul dedicated his life to wiping out Indians. He learned the plains and how to track and hunt from a succession of scouts and mountain men, until he found the cavalry made a business of the thing that was uppermost in his mind.

And then Paul found himself at Fort Desolation, entrusted with keeping a passel of redskins alive when there was barely enough food in the fort for the handful of troopers, their wives, and their children.

Paul inspected his scouting party. Seven lonely men

to prod the desert dryness for three days in hopes of keeping the Apaches away. Then there would be another three days . . . and another . . . and another . . . if relief came before the food ran out.

Paul glanced over his shoulder at the clot of well-fed Comanche scouts under the shade in front of the sutler's store.

"Sarge, ain't we gonna take an Indian scout?"

That was Corporal Devon. He set such store by the noble redman that he had taken an Indian woman for a wife.

Paul spotted one of the Comanches repairing the buckskin lacing on his shield, a shield decorated with hanks of hair. And one long red tress had obviously not been lifted from an Apache head. Paul remembered his mother's death and made a grim decision. He turned to the corporal.

"Yes, Devon, we're going to take a scout."

He turned back toward the Comanches.

"Hey, you! Runny Nose!" He sighted his finger at the one with the shield. "Time to earn your grub."

As Paul watched the Indian push to his feet, he tested the delicately edged knife at his belt. Runny Nose's hair was blue-black and long enough for a good handhold. Ward of the Government or not, by the time the scouting party got back to Fort Desolation there would be one less Injun to feed.

The writer would have to push aside the temptation to describe Paul's maturing years under the tutelage of scouts and mountain men; after all, his military rank establishes the fact that he has become proficient at his trade. So far as the coming conflict is concerned, the core of the background information is Paul's memory of seeing his mother scalped. In the above version, the motivation is hidden in the flat, objective statement, "Paul remembered his mother's death and made a grim decision." Let's rewrite that paragraph and have the incident take place in Paul's mind as a living incident:

Paul spotted one of the Comanches repairing the buckskin lacing on his shield, a shield decorated with hanks of hair. And one long red tress had obviously not been lifted from an Apache head. Paul closed his eyes and found himself cowering in the Conestoga, peering out from under the wagon sheet, but he could not make out the color of his mother's hair as she knelt beside his father's limp body. Then she jumped to her feet and ran away from the wagon. The Indian wheeled his pony in an arc to intercept her and scoop her from the ground. Before he could rear the horse to a stop they were only a few feet from the wagon. Paul heard his mother's husky breath, "Lie terribly still, Paul darling."

The Comanche gathered her hair in his hand. His knife flashed in the sun as he traced a delicate circle around the top of her head with the point. The hair came away with a faint squeaking, wrenching sound, and the loose skin of his mother's forehead wrinkled bloodily down over her eyes as she sank writhing to the ground. The brave rode away with a screaming hoot, waving his dripping trophy overhead. It *was* red!

Paul McAdams opened his eyes and turned to Corporal Devon.

"Yes, Devon, we're going to take an Indian scout with us."

The reader has now seen Paul's decision from the inside out; he has been with the character during the motivation and decision for his future in the story. In using this technique, the writer must work his character against his story until he develops a feel for the events which must be highlighted by viewpoint.

To a certain extent, the depth of characterization must be determined by the type of story the writer is producing. By its very nature, a character story is concerned with the development and evolvement of an individual within the framework of the dramatic situation. Such a story must penetrate deeper into the life of the individual than, for example, a situation comedy which is peopled with stereotypes and has as its purpose entertainment by way of displaying social foibles.

Application of the principle of single viewpoint gives the writer a good rule of thumb: *Present only as much of the viewpoint character's life as he is aware of during that portion of his life which is involved in your story.* If you stick to this, you can't go wrong. Everything you present will have a bearing on the drama at hand; it will either happen to the character during the course of the story or it will occur to him as a result of the story's events. You will have no excess wordage to detract from the progress and effect of your narrative.

Most successful writers find that their first probings into a story are in reality the process of getting acquainted with their characters. Not being committed to the irretrievability of serial publication, most of today's writers can proceed to the drama along with its characters, after they have evolved from the creative process. Some writers begin by writing a rather full character sketch, a sort of personal purging during which they eliminate nonessentials and distill their central characters. Out of this process emerges the individual who is capable of creating the drama in which the writer involves him, a character who is no more or no less than he needs to be.

How much description?

How much description of the viewpoint character should there be? The answer is so simple that it sounds sarcastic: use as much description of your viewpoint character as your story requires. In a story which demands that a hero or a heroine have certain physical characteristics, those characteristics—or their effects— must be displayed to make the character seem real and plausible. It takes a red suit and a white beard to make a child believe in Santa Claus, so old Saint Nick had jolly well better not show up without these things.

Some audiences virtually demand descriptions of their viewpoint characters. For example, the readers of women's magazines have an inherent interest in fashions; they like to know what the heroines they read about are wearing. However, this does not mean that the writer needs to step out of viewpoint to insert a block of descriptive material. The feminine character who sees herself in a mirror or a plate glass window and thinks about her appearance, who pays attention to the selection of her wardrobe, and who compares her own appearance to that of other women will seem a perfectly credible person to the female reader who engages in these same activities every day.

Description for the sake of description has no place

in a narrative. Actually, detailed physical description of the viewpoint character can be an obstacle to reader identification. I am ready and eager to identify with a male viewpoint character who proves himself by thought and deed to be generous, intelligent, and exceedingly attractive to the opposite sex. However, when I learn that this person is twenty-five years of age, redheaded, six-foot-four, and weighs two hundred and ten without an ounce of fat, my mind begins to pall at allowing my obviously inadequate body to join such a physical paragon vicariously in any kind of activities. I conducted an experiment which points up the extent to which the reader during the reading process becomes a hero in his own image.

In a story in a publication directed toward a youthful audience, I found not a single word of physical description of the heroine, nor was her age mentioned. I got a hundred copies of the magazine and, with the cooperation of a high school English department, had them distributed to a hundred students in the sixteen-to-eighteen age group. They read the story. Then the magazines were taken away and the students were asked to write a character sketch of the heroine.

Only one reader, a sixteen-year-old boy, noted that there was no information about the girl's age or physical appearance. Thirteen included no details of physical appearance in their sketches, although one of these said, "Alice has trouble with her skin." (Alice's problem was that she was a well-traveled newcomer in a cliquish community.) Each of the remaining eighty-six students was able to visualize the character sufficiently to include some physical description. In general, the girls were more detailed than the boys.

The descriptive details included by the girls generally pertained to themselves. Almost universally, the girls who included age pegged Alice at one or two years older than themselves. The heroine did things which most of the girls would have liked to be doing but could not, presumably because they were too young. Consequently, they mentally placed such activities in the future and assumed the character to be older than they.

The descriptive details included by the boys were more difficult to trace, but those that could be pinpointed had been transferred from sisters and girl friends. Two teachers found themselves. One descriptive bit was a puzzler, "Alice was just a little bit gray-headed," until the teacher remembered that this boy's mother, a woman of perhaps forty, had salt-and-pepper hair. She was indeed "very beautiful," but hardly comparable to Alice, who achieved her goal by winning a dance contest in her bare feet.

Absence of physical description of the principal character is not an uncommon thing. For example, you can read *Treasure Island* from cover to cover, and you won't find a trace of Jim Hawkins' appearance. This has made it easy for generation after generation of readers of assorted sizes, shapes, and ages to visualize themselves in the search for pirate treasure.

The requirement of a given story for description of its hero or heroine can be determined by subjecting the contemplated details to two tests. First, look at each detail from within the viewpoint character. If it is necessary for him to see himself in order to prove something to himself—and to the reader—let him see himself. If a certain detail is essential to the development of the character, to prove the character to the reader, let that detail show. Use your blue pencil on anything which does not meet one of these two criteria.

What's in a name?

On the cold black and white of the printed page, a rose by any other name would definitely *not* smell as sweet, because a rose is a rose is a rose. Correct use of characters' names in relation to your viewpoint character is vital to establishing a relationship between the reader and the characters you are portraying.

If you expect your reader to become sympathetic to your character and to feel that he knows him, establish that character on a first-name basis with your reader. This is rather the same in fiction as it is in real life: You never feel that you know someone very well if you don't know his first name, if you can call him only by his title, "Mister," "Doctor," "Professor," "Captain," or whatever. For example:

> Mrs. Jonathan C. Clegg's first warning of trouble came with a faint whooshing across the back of her neck, so close that the sound felt like a tiny puff of wind. She turned toward the dull thud that sounded from the wall and saw, still quivering, the dart from the blowgun which was supposed to be in the trophy room. Its end pointed out into the blackness beyond the open window.
>
> Mrs. Clegg collapsed to the floor, not by virtue of

quick thinking or well-trained reflexes but because her knees turned to water. Mrs. Clegg was experienced in fear. At twenty, while on her honeymoon, she had faced a charging tiger in India, to prove that she was worthy of Jonathan C. Clegg. The next year she had dropped a berserk elephant at her very feet and had then been asked by the Tanganzis to lead the hunt for a man-killing lion. But never before had she experienced such fear as now froze her throat so she couldn't even scream for help.

Now Mrs. Clegg was the hunted. There were fourteen house guests, all Mr. Jonathan C. Clegg's relatives, each with a small fortune to gain by Mr. Clegg's will—if only she were out of the way. Mrs. Clegg rolled over on her face to smother her scream in the rug.

From this opening, Mrs. Clegg seems to be a pretty cold fish, even if she is terror-stricken. She may attract the curious, but she is not likely to acquire a substantial following of sympathetic vicarious participants. Notice how we can pick up a certain warmth for the character with no other alteration of the text than changing the names:

Sarah Clegg's first warning of trouble came with a faint whooshing across the back of her neck, so close that the sound felt like a tiny puff of wind. She turned toward the dull thud that sounded from the wall and saw, still quivering, the dart from the blowgun which was supposed to be in the trophy room. Its end pointed out into the blackness beyond the open window.

Sarah collapsed to the floor, not by virtue of quick thinking or well-trained reflexes but because her knees turned to water. Sarah was experienced in fear. At twenty, while on her honeymoon, she had faced a charging tiger in India, to prove that she was worthy of Jonathan C. Clegg. The next year she had dropped a berserk elephant at her very feet and had then been asked by the Tanganzis to lead the hunt for a man-killing lion. But never before had she experienced such fear as now froze her throat so she couldn't even scream for help.

Now Sarah was the hunted. There were fourteen house guests, all Jonathan's relatives, each with a small fortune to gain by Jonathan's will—if only she were out of the way. Sarah rolled over on her face to smother her scream in the rug.

The next rule in the viewpoint name game is to have all other characters occupy a logical position with respect to the viewpoint character by name and other identifying designations. Let's illustrate this with a young viewpoint character named Vivian Carter Metz. Vivian was named after his maternal grandfather, and he hates it all the way:

Vivian Carter Metz waited at the bottom of the stairs for his father, Mr. Herbert W. Metz. Finally Mr. Metz came down.

"Son, shouldn't you be on your way to school?"

"Dad, I just wanted to ask you if I can change my name this year, now that I'm going into the fourth grade. Gee, can I? Can I tell the teacher it's just plain Carter Metz? Can I, Dad?"

Vivian felt Mr. Metz's hand smoothing his hair with that too-soft touch and knew the answer before he spoke. "Now, we've been through this before. Your grandfather was a fine old gentleman, a governor of

this state. Some day you'll be proud to carry his name."
Mr. Metz gave his son a little push toward the door.
"Off with you, Vivian."

Vivian could see from Mrs. Metz' face that she was
not going to be of any help. "Now, Vivian, remember:
We're not going to have any fighting this year." That
was all she said.

Vivian dashed out of the front door to keep them
from seeing the tears that he could feel coming. "I wish
he'd been a murderer, that's what I wish. Then they
wouldn't make me keep his name!"

Once at the sidewalk Vivian walked slowly, hoping he
would get to school late enough that he wouldn't have
to spend any time on the playground. But he was not
slow enough.

Just as he came opposite the Fosters' house, his classmate William G. Foster came out.

"Good morning, Miss Metz," said William as he fell
into step beside Vivian.

Vivian felt his hands beginning to tremble. He
shoved them into his pockets and walked faster. William ran to get far enough ahead that he could turn
around and walk backwards in front of him.

"Viv-ian 'za sissy name—Viv-ian 'za sissy name—
Viv-ian 'za sissy name . . ."

From across the street Vivian heard Tobias T.
Catlin's shrill voice taking up the chant. He felt his
hands balling up hard in his pockets. He took them out.
He wished that Mr. and Mrs. Metz were there and
could see how it was. A guy just had to fight with a
name like Vivian.

The above narrative is (with one exception) in
Vivian's viewpoint, but the references to the other characters are not. The result is a warped perspective which
does not give a true feeling of the relationships between

characters. A boy simply does not think of his mother and father as "Mr." and "Mrs." William G. Foster and Tobias T. Catlin would be "Bill" and "Toby"—or one of them might even be called "Wart Nose"—but hardly "William" and "Tobias," to say nothing of the use of middle initials. In the above, if "Bill Foster" had come out of the Fosters' house, it would not have been necessary to use the awkward "his classmate" to be sure the reader understood that it was not the head of the Foster household.

The proper relationship is achieved by projecting yourself into your character's viewpoint and referring to those persons about him as *he* would think of them. This not only reflects a more natural situation, but as a dividend it can also show your character's attitude toward other participants in the drama without your having to tell the reader. Your hero may call his boss "J. C." and introduce him formally as "Mr. Rowsome," but he may think of him privately as "Old Skinflint." This is a part of presentation from his viewpoint.

I mentioned that the above narrative sample is in Vivian's viewpoint with one exception. This exception demonstrates a common difficulty. Note the sentence, "Mr. Metz gave his son a little push toward the door." Vivian would not logically think of himself as "his son"; this phraseology would be a natural part of the father's viewpoint outlook. The use of a preposition referring to the viewpoint character would get around the trouble in this particular case and put that portion of the sentence into proper viewpoint perspective: ". . . gave him a little push . . ." Such illogical character designation tends to lessen the effectiveness of any viewpoint. It gives one's writing a general fuzziness.

Going back to the coolness which is created by the use of titles alone and by failing to let the reader know a character's first name, it is possible to use these devices to create a subtle plant of villainy. If the first name of a character is never revealed, if he is always referred to only by his title and/or surname, the reader will not be at all surprised when he turns out to be the guy who wears the black hat.

VI

MAKING YOUR READER
TAKE PART

————•◦•————

A good fiction writer's art is in making the printed page disappear, in making his paper person so real that the reading world will go into mourning upon the publication of a notice such as, "It is with a heavy heart that I take up my pen to write these the last words in which I shall ever record the singular gifts by which my friend Mr. Sherlock Holmes was distinguished." ("The Final Problem," *Memoirs of Sherlock Holmes*.)

Making the reader come alive as a character out of the book he reads is accomplished within the reader's heart and mind, not on the surface of the page he is reading. The process is akin to hypnosis as the reader's consciousness leaves the page before him to join in the world of imagination the character he is reading about. We have discussed the necessity for the writer to become involved in his story to such an extent that he can project himself wholeheartedly into his character, and we have shown some of the techniques by which the reader is led into vicarious participation in the story via viewpoint. Now it is time to get down to cases on some of the finer details of the doing.

As is usually the case, it is easier to analyze the methods which have proved successful than it is to accomplish the task they perform. Capturing the reader is basically a three-step process: First, the reader is provided with a means by which he can sympathize with the character; then he is placed in emotional suspense by involvement in the situation; and, finally, he is kept in this involved state by the impact of a continuing flow of cause-effect relationship.

Getting the reader's sympathy

In previous chapters we discussed how to build motivation in viewpoint and the fact that a minimal amount of physical description can often be an additional aid to reader identification. But reader identification alone is not enough to get the reader off the printed page. The reader must sympathize with the character; and in order for this to happen, you must establish a common bond between the reader and the character you are portraying. Normally, this is best accomplished by showing, *in viewpoint,* some universal feeling, reaction, or desire which the character and the reader have in common.

Let's look at an example:

Connie Rader had been married to Ted for almost a year before she gave a second thought to his casual question as to whether she liked to go camping. They had been on a picnic at the time, and the people in the tents and trailers looked as if they were having a wonderful time; besides, Connie was so much in love that it was very hard to see beyond Ted's blue eyes and blond hair.

She was no less in love as they started to get ready to go on their first vacation, but the heap of camping equipment in the garage was beginning to assume alarming proportions beside their compact car. Ted made a big secret of their destination.

"I'm not sure we can get permission yet, and I wouldn't want to disappoint you."

On the day before they were to leave, he skidded into the driveway with a rented luggage trailer bouncing along behind. He was waving a piece of paper. "I got it! I got it! I got it!"

Connie looked up from trying to repack ten cubic feet of nesting aluminum camp cookware into two cubic feet of box.

"We got official permission!" He was dancing around her now, rattling the paper. "*We* are going to be the first white men to explore Savahu Cave."

Connie stood up and stretched her sweat shirt tightly across her chest. "I'm going to have to have a talk with you about sex."

But Ted didn't stop talking. ". . . the very first! It's the chance of a lifetime."

Savahu Cave, it seemed, was a mysterious taboo cave, tucked away in an obscure mountain canyon on the Pokito Indian Reservation. No white man had ever seen its entrance, much less explored it. The cave was only a day's drive—plus three days by pack mule—and they were going to have fun.

We are well on our way to establishing the situation. However, unless our reader is female and happens to be pretty thoroughly fed up with camping, we do not yet have a common bond between Connie and the reader. We may have a smattering of reader identification—if our reader has ever been frustrated by trying to pack one of those nesting camp cooking outfits—but we do not yet have sympathy for the character. To establish that bond of sympathy, we will introduce Connie's problem with a reaction virtually universal among women, and present in a fairly high percentage of the male sex.

First of all, however, to achieve a properly tight weave to the plot of our story, we need to go back into the text and plant something to make the next incident appear as a natural development of the story rather than as something the writer has contrived. We can forecast the future by adding a bit of elaboration upon the camping equipment at the end of the second paragraph of the example: ". . . compact car—everything from a snakebite kit to a tent that looked big enough to house a circus."

Now for the next development:

It developed that all three mules were to carry camping gear. Connie, Ted, and an impassive Indian named Okeepah walked a tortuous trail which stretched up the face of a cliff like an eyebrow. By mid-morning when they stopped to drink a thermos of coffee, the tops of the tall pines on the canyon floor had shrunk to a dim green haze far, far below.

"I've always wanted to spit a mile," Ted said.

Connie tried to push her back into the cliff behind her. "I hate spitting."

They had barely started walking again when one of the mules let out a wild bray fit to inspire the *Grand*

Canyon Suite and scampered off up the trail, scattering camping gear behind. Ted swore loudly and dove to keep their cooking outfit from bouncing over the edge of the trail. Okeepah grabbed Connie and literally shoved her on up the trail a few yards. He looked as if he had come face to face with an evil spirit.

Connie leaned against the cliff to catch her breath. "What was that all about?"

"Savahu!" Okeepah pointed behind them. His eyes were terror-stricken pinpoints.

Connie became aware of a vicious whirring sound and saw a large snake coiled by the cliff, inches from where she had been. Its head stood up, waving gently at her, as if beckoning. She could see the sun gleaming off the slimy-looking yellowish-white of its underside. Wavy lines came between her and the snake, and the sky filled with tiny black dots as she looked away to keep from fainting. She fought back the sickness that came into her throat.

"What did you call it?"

"Savahu—rattlesnake."

"That—that's the name of the cave."

"That's why," Okeepah said.

"Come on, you all," called Ted. "We've got to get this stuff gathered up and repack the mule or we'll never get to the cave."

And so, we have established a common bond of sympathy between our character and our reader through an almost universal emotion—the fear of snakes. If such a bond is not established, the size of the reading audience will be limited. All readers cannot be expected to throb to the story of Cinderella—and there may even be a few hardy souls who are not afraid of rattlesnakes.

The element of universality which forms the common bond with the character can be a simple trait—like the love of food, a tendency to eat too much, which creates a weight problem for so many; or laziness, which causes most of us to procrastinate; or the mere ability to feel pain; or a desire for security. These are characteristics the reader will understand because he has them in common with the character portrayed. He will understand troubles and conflicts stemming from these universal qualities, because they are almost daily sources of his own troubles and conflicts; he will thus sympathize with the story character.

No personality trait should exist in the abstract, apart from the main line of the story. Each quality should justify its existence as a part of the plot or in the development of the character. You can bet your old hackneyed bottom dollar that Connie is going to have trouble because of her fear of snakes, and any rotund young man with an appetite is likely to find his girl friend dating a slender young tennis player.

Sometimes the writer can inadvertently destroy his character's bond with the reader. I remember one story in which my character was named Christian von Reinhardt. It came back with the editorial comment, "We like your story. We are particularly interested in the authenticity of its background. But we don't feel that your character has a sufficiently common touch to achieve reader identification." I was stymied. The one thing I thought I had achieved was a universally understandable character. In fact, I had given him a rather hoity-toity name to try to remove him from the common herd. But maybe that was it!

I retyped the story. The only alteration was to change my character's name to John Gardener. (I couldn't think of one that was more down-to-earth.) In my note to the editor I said I had rewritten the story and hoped that the character was now on a more universal level. Right back came a letter—a nice thin one with an airmail stamp: "Your story now has just the touch we are looking for! You did an excellent job of revision."

The writer's sympathy for his character may be so complete that he may take it for granted that the reader feels the same as he does and forget to show the motivation for it in his character's viewpoint. Sometimes this happens because the real motivation is part of the writer's personality but has not been transferred to the character; sometimes it is in the background development of the character as it exists in the writer's mind rather than on paper. It is well to try to pinpoint the exact spot in the first draft of your manuscript where you have established reader sympathy for your character—just to be sure you have done so.

Sometimes the nature of the character complicates the writer's task. I remember a story I wrote about a muleskinner. He had to be rough and tough, but he also had to have the reader's sympathy. By the end of five thousand words I had my story, but I also realized that my character didn't have a ghost of a chance of penetrating the reader until virtually the end of the yarn. I poked around at the thing for two days. Nothing jelled: He couldn't send his mother a birthday present; he was an orphan. There just weren't any little old ladies to help across the street in Virginia City, Montana, in 1863. To heck with it!

That night I went to a wrestling match. I saw a wrestler who must have tipped the scales at only a few pounds under half a ton going into a dressing room. In his great hand, he was carrying a Manchester terrier that looked about the size of a dime. The light dawned, and I turned around and went home.

I needed an identifiable breed of dog that could have been in Virginia City, Montana, in 1863. My encyclopedia said the Pekingese went back as early as 2000 B.C. By morning I had my story through the typewriter again. A few people had to get shot in a saloon brawl during the natural course of the story's beginning. I changed one of them to a Chinese laundryman who had smuggled one of the sacred temple dogs out of Peking. My muleskinner took this laundryman's whimpering, orphaned Pekingese home with him. Then, at a later critical point, instead of having the horses sound an alarm, I let Foo Chow do it. My character's rough edges were honed off, and the story sold the first trip out.

Another almost sure route to reader sympathy for a character is imperfection. As Tennyson put it, "He is all fault who hath no fault at all. For who loves me must have a touch of earth." Each of us has some kind of an imperfection and a feeling of inferiority resulting from it. If you search your character's viewpoint, you will usually find his "imperfection," weakness, flaw, or fault. It may be physical—a mole, a slightly crooked nose, a limp (like Philip Carey in *Of Human Bondage*), a stutter; emotional—the inability to express himself, self-consciousness, extreme shyness; mental— a sense of inferiority, established in his background, of course; or any other characteristic which makes him something of an underdog and creates a sympathetic bond with the reader.

Portrayal of imperfection by way of viewpoint is the writer's method of making the "juggler's slip": If a highly skilled juggler appears on stage and executes a flawless performance he will, as they say in sports, "make it look easy." His performance will be really appreciated only by those who know enough about juggling to realize how difficult his feat is. However, if he makes a bobble, his spectators will know that it is not easy; everyone in the audience will, in effect, be right up there on the stage with him, pulling for him to be able to complete his act successfully.

Emotional suspense

No matter how vital the message or how large the struggle he wants to portray, the fiction writer must never forget one fact: *Were it not for people, there would be no struggles about which to write.*

A dramatic situation may involve great social forces, vast armies, mighty nations, ideologies which vie for the control of millions of people, but whatever its magnitude, the meaning and force of the situation are best transmitted to the reader through the viewpoint of a *single* participant. No struggle is so great that it cannot be concentrated in the passions of one person: The religious zealot who adheres to his cause to the point of martyrdom serves as a representative of his spiritual faith; the adolescent who joins the age-old rebellion to live a free and independent existence, to gain recognition, to wear the latest fad—long hair or short, tight pants or bell-bottomed trousers—is a manifestation of his generation.

Passion is the root of every human struggle. No matter how sweeping or how trivial the cause, in the final analysis the person who joins it is moved to do so by an individual, intimate, emotional experience. This fact provides both the drama of a situation and the means by which it can be created—or recreated—within the reader. The portrayal of that emotional experience creates the suspense which gives meaning to the drama.

Individual emotional evolvement erupts from the personality of the principal character, dictating the role he is to play. The situation challenges a trait of character and results in emotional conflict *within* the individual. This is the story's reason for being. The story takes on both meaning and suspense as this internal conflict is communicated to the reader. Let's synopsize a familiar example—de Maupassant's story, "A Piece of String"—to see how it works:

> Maître Hauchecome, of Breaute, went to Goderville for market day. Hauchecome saw a piece of string on the ground and, being a *miserly* person, picked it up. As he did so, he noticed that he had been observed by M. Malandrain, a local harness-maker whom he *hated* because of previous business differences. He was

ashamed to be seen picking up a piece of string out of the dirt, so he concealed it. Then it developed that a citizen had lost a pocketbook. Malandrain accused Hauchecome of picking up the pocketbook and hiding it. Hauchecome denied this and showed the piece of string, but no one believed him. Eventually the lost pocketbook was returned by someone else. However, people continued to believe Hauchecome had had something to do with the pocketbook, and he died from the *shame* of the accusation as he continued in vain to protest his innocence.

Note that the story had its beginning in an act motivated by Maître Hauchecome's basic trait of character, miserliness. Had he not been "economical like a true Norman" and "thought that everything useful ought to be picked up," the story would never have started, because Hauchecome would not have picked up the piece of string. When he was observed in the act, his basic trait of miserliness came into conflict with the emotionally motivated feeling of shame, a bit of vanity which is a part of all of us in one form or another. Shame continued to motivate him to the very end.

If this facet of character had not been a part of Hauchecome, he would have paid no attention to Malandrain; he would not have attempted to conceal the fact that he had picked up a piece of string. The dramatic situation could not have evolved. . . . If he had not felt shame, it would have made no difference that others continued to accuse him after the pocketbook was found. There would have been no story.

The story is successful because every reader can remember having felt ashamed at being caught in some niggardly act and consequently can identify with Hauchecome in his situation. Emotional suspense is achieved because de Maupassant never released his character from his emotional state. If at any point in the development of the story—from its beginning which showed Hauchecome picking up a piece of string, to the ending, with his death resulting from this act—Hauchecome had lost his sense of shame, there could have been no story. In fact, without this trait, there would have been no reason to begin the story.

Note that the character's emotional reaction also plays a part in establishing the story's plausibility. Had Hauchecome been observed by a complete stranger, his reaction would have been highly improbable. But he *hated* the harness-maker, and so it seems quite credible that he would be ashamed.

Examine the most successful stories and dramas, and you will find a core of emotional suspense at the heart of virtually all, whether it be a short story with a simple, basic plot line like "A Piece of String" or the more complicated dramatic development of a complex character like Macbeth. Macbeth began his role as a brave man of honor and integrity. Prodded by Lady Macbeth, Macbeth let ambition challenge the better side of his character, and he committed his first crime to gain a throne. From that point on, Shakespeare never released Macbeth from a state of emotional suspense; each flicker of hope brought more fear to the very end.

The basic pattern of drama is so deceptively simple that most inexperienced writers tend to lose its impact in intricacies of characterization and incident which are beside the point. Drama creates itself within man: The principal character commits an act which stems from a character trait. Internal emotional conflict results; drama lasts as long as the individual is kept in a state of emotional suspense.

If the same emotional state prevails to the end of the drama, the story's emotional line is simple and its impact upon the reader is likely to be stronger than the impact which results from a changing emotional state. If the same emotional state is not maintained within the character to the end of the drama, the writer must be certain that the transition from one emotional state to the next carries *both* the character and the reader.

Maintaining emotional suspense

Viewpoint is the surest path to maintaining emotional suspense and to communicating the emotional quality of your story to the reader, whether the emotional pattern be simple or complex. In reality, it becomes a matter of properly reflecting the everyday cause-and-effect pattern of our lives. As inevitably as day follows night, the pattern repeats its cycle: Stimulus—emotional reaction—action . . . stimulus—emotional reaction—action . . . over and over and over again. Let's see how it might have happened to you:

> *Stimulus*: You reached the point in dressing to go out to an important affair that you were ready to put on your suit or dress. You went to the closet and removed the garment, took off the protective bag in which you brought it

home from the dry cleaner's, and there—right before your eyes—was a large grease spot which had not even been there when you sent it to the cleaner.

Emotional reaction: Anger

Action: You went to the telephone, dialed the dry cleaner's number, and proceeded to discuss quality of workmanship with whoever answered the phone.

Stimulus: "I'm afraid I can't do anything for you. All of our complaints are handled through our central office. You will have to call them."

Emotional reaction: Extreme anger.

Action: You telephoned the central office of your dry cleaner and finally reached someone who admitted to being in charge of complaints. You told him about the grease spot.

Stimulus: "If you will look at the top of your receipt, you will note that it says: 'All complaints must be registered on Service Complaint Form 1492 at the time cleaning is delivered.' That notice is also plainly posted behind the counter. Now, if you will bring your duplicate copy of Form 1492 to my office, we will be glad to start proceedings for an adjustment."

Emotional reaction: Frustrated rage.

Action: You delivered an impassioned discourse on the dubious ancestry of dry cleaners in general and your dry cleaner in particular.

That should be sufficient to show the naked outline of a familiar pattern. Notice the interlocking relationship between action and stimulus.

Once this pattern of cause and effect has been set into motion, each emotional reaction produces an action by the viewpoint character which triggers another stimulus which causes emotional reaction which sets off another action which calls for another stimulus which results in more emotional reaction . . . and as long as the principal character continues to react he remains in a state of emotional suspense and the drama continues. Anything in your text which does not contribute to the stimulus, the emotional reaction, or the action evolving about your principal character is extraneous to the emotional line—and hence the drama—of your story, regardless of what other function it might perform.

We will reproduce a sample from a story we have used previously to demonstrate how this pattern works. The example is coded as follows to show the steps which are a part of sustaining emotional suspense:

Parentheses ( ) = stimulus
Italics = emotional reaction
Roman type = action
Brackets [ ] = material which does not contribute directly to stimulus, emotional reaction, or action

[Martha Treece turned on the radio and curled up in the big chair for another] (night of waiting) [for Henry.] (She knew that somebody had to go when people got sick, but it seemed that it always had to be Henry.)

Martha picked up her book from the coffee table. (*Night of Terror.*) *She smiled* (at the picture of the screaming woman on the book jacket.) *Thank heaven* (for mystery stories!)

("In spite of Detective Fry's not believing her, Carmen was sure after overhearing the telephone conversation that she was next. 'She knows too much,' the grating voice had said. So she decided to hide behind the drapes in her room, instead of going to bed. . . .")

(Martha heard the distant wail of a screaming siren) and looked up at the clock. (Only eight-thirty.) *What if it were an accident? And what if Henry had to—* She turned the radio louder and went back to the book to keep from thinking about it.

("Carmen felt the dusty drapes tickling her nose as the French windows opened. All she could see through the tiny slit was a shadow, but that shadow was enough. It was a hand, holding a gun. If she—")

(The music stopped abruptly.)

("We interrupt this program to bring you a bulletin. The Penrock Supermarket has been held up at gunpoint . . .")

Martha felt the pain of her teeth catching her lower lip. (Penrock was only two blocks away.)

(". . . identified from photographs as Joseph McQuerry, alias Mack Joseph, one of the ten most wanted men, the bandit was last seen on foot, carrying a brown paper bag. He is armed and dangerous. He—")

Martha switched off the radio and listened (to the creaking whisper of the empty house.) *Now she wished she would hear another siren. At least she would know the police were around.* (The front door!) *A mist of perspiration gathered on her forehead.* Had the front door squeaked? But she had locked it. She loosened her grip on the book and smoothed the crumpled page.

("Carmen felt the dusty drapes tickling her nose as the French windows opened. All—")

A thousand prickles ran across Martha's scalp (as she heard a man clear his throat. Then there was the whispering silence again,) and all she could hear was *the blood pumping in her temples.* (She picked out the plink of the leaky kitchen faucet) and realized that what she had heard must have been water gurgling down the drain. She wiped her palm down the leg of her slacks and *winced from her digging fingernails.* She forced her eyes back to the book.

("Carmen felt the dusty drapes—")

(Then Martha heard the crackling of paper. *A brown paper bag!*) She looked up, squarely into the big round blue muzzle of a gun.

In the writing, the pattern becomes less naked and less easy to define than the retrospective analysis of an encounter with the dry cleaner. Most of the emotional reactions are projected into the reader's mind by way of the character's mind, which allows the reader to infer the character's emotional reaction by experiencing it vicariously, rather than by being told about it; in other cases, the reader is given the physical reaction associated with the emotion (the prickling scalp, for example); and in still other cases, the emotional reaction is expressed in the character's action (wiping her perspiring palm). Let's examine some of the details:

In the beginning, a minimum of wordage is used to set the situation. Note that even narrative material can be sprinkled with phrases contributory to or foreshadowing the stimulus, like "night of waiting." And it was not by accident that Martha was reading a mystery story, concerning someone in a situation comparable to her own, entitled *Night of Terror,* with a picture of a screaming woman on the book jacket.

Her first act was to pick up the book. The title and the illustration served as stimuli, and her first emotional reaction was mild, portrayed by a smile and an expression of relief at having mystery stories to read. Note that each action does not have to take place in front of the reader's eyes. If we were to strip the emotional suspense formula down to its bare outline at this point, it would go something like this:

Action:	Martha picked up a book from her coffee table and looked at it.
Stimulus:	It was a mystery story entitled *Night of Terror* with a picture of a screaming woman on the book jacket.
Emotional reaction:	Pleasure and relief at having something to do while her husband was away.
Action:	She began to read.
Stimulus:	The story was about a woman whose life was in danger. While she was reading, Martha heard a siren in the distance.

The use of the right viewpoint can provide the reader with knowledge of the character's actions without the necessity for direct statement. It is not necessary to say something like, "Martha looked at her book and saw . . ." or "Martha began to read." Being in her mind, the reader knows that she looked at the book and that she began to read, because he sees what she saw and reads what she read. Similarly, an emotional reaction does not have to be told or described; it can be communicated by a speech, an action ("She smiled"), or even a thought ("Thank heaven") .

The particular passage Martha was reading was not only a stimulus to heighten the reader's emotional reaction, but having her read it over and over again was a way of showing that she was becoming more and more wrought up—an experience with which every reader can identify.

When she heard the siren, her emotional reaction was mild alarm, expressed by her concern about Henry, and her action was to do something to keep from thinking about it. This follows the emotional suspense pattern.

Note toward the end of the example, as the character gets deeper into the emotional state and the reader is reacting with her, the pattern was varied: Martha's scalp prickled to allow the reader to anticipate being scared. This was pre-planned. The man with the gun had been forecast by the passage from the book; he had been created as a part of Martha's situation. It was inevitable that he should appear. And a final point: The brown paper bag had been planted in advance, so that it would serve as both a stimulus and an emotional reaction when it appeared. This is an old movie trick which, if well done, usually brings a gasp from the audience.

Applying the pattern

Now for the actual application of this pattern for maintaining emotional suspense:

Suppose the writer sits down and says, "Now I am going to apply the pattern to obtain emotional suspense. Here is my first stimulus, my first emotional reaction, and my first action. And here is my second stimulus . . ." I can guarantee that the writing will go miserably, and the resulting story will be as stiff as a cigar store Indian.

To apply this pattern successfully, you must realize that it is an analysis of a natural, inevitable way of life; that it is to be forgotten by the writer until it is the right time to use it. The writer should first project himself into his viewpoint character and live the story onto paper. The real use for the pattern comes after the first draft is written, after the writer has created his character, learned of his traits and his conflicts, and knows how he acts and how he feels. *After* you have your story on paper and can feel its emotional drive, then test every word, phrase, and paragraph, each incident, stimulus, action, and reaction against the pattern to see that what you actually have on paper is consistent with your intent. Here is a checklist:

1. Have you established—by showing it in viewpoint—the trait of your character upon which his first emotional response is based?
2. Have you shown your character experiencing a situation which will adequately stimulate that emotional response?
3. Have you placed the initial stimulus within your character as a living experience, even though it may have occurred in his past?

4. When the emotional reaction is a conflict between two emotional states—fear of snakes *versus* love of one's husband, for example—have you shown the development of this conflict within your character?

5. Is *each* stimulus adequate motivation for the emotional reaction it causes?

6. Is *each* of your viewpoint character's emotional responses shown from within the character?

7. Does each action naturally follow from its causative emotional reaction?

8. Are all "surprises" adequately forecast or foreshadowed so that the chain of circumstances in your story does not appear contrived?

9. Does each action lead logically or inevitably to the next stimulus so that the narrative is an uninterrupted flow?

10. If there is a change in the viewpoint character's emotional state, is the change adequately motivated by the stimulus and shown from within the character?

11. Is *every word* of anything which does not directly contribute to the viewpoint character's stimulus, emotional reaction, and action *absolutely necessary*?

When you have worked on your story until you can give an affirmative answer to each of the above questions, the chances are good that your story will create effective emotional suspense.

Emotional flow

Like most artists, fiction writers strive primarily to create an emotional experience in their audience. But writers have an advantage over many other kinds of artists in that writing exists in time rather than space, as does a painting or a piece of sculpture. A painting, for example, is there to be seen all at once and, for that reason, the artist must attempt to create its emotional impact on sight. On the other hand, by its very nature, written material must be read during a time sequence, and the writer has the opportunity to build its emotional impact by means of a logical emotional sequence.

It is important for the writer to capitalize on the advantage which this situation gives him, an advantage greatly aided by the fact that emotion is contagious. By means of viewpoint, the writer can lead his reader through a series of emotional experiences, gradually building to his climax as the reader becomes more and more involved by vicarious participation. Some of the emotional experiences may miss, since any particular reader's personal experience may not allow him to participate in a given emotional reaction; however, if the writer maintains a smooth emotional flow which does not distract the reader from the state of emotional suspense, the reader will gloss over a few extraneous emotional experiences much as we gloss over the words we do not know when we are reading. He will continue in the emotional state because of the general emotional context, without actually participating in those experiences which are alien to his nature.

The writer's part in viewpoint

One of viewpoint's greatest uses is in making it easier for the writer to keep to his role as the creator without intruding into the drama he is creating. We have already discussed the fact that the practice of engaging in direct address to the reader is no longer considered good technique, no matter how frequently you find examples in the "old classics."

Most novices experience difficulty in subordinating their own personalities. The beginning writer knows that he should individualize his story, put something of himself into it. He does not yet realize that this is almost inevitable as a part of his characterization and in the philosophy which he reflects in his writing, so he is tempted to side remarks, criticisms, bits of moralizing, opinion, and other forms of editorial comment entirely out of keeping with the character he is creating. This is often superfluous elaboration. For example:

David Copperton left his Madison Avenue office and hurried toward the Happy Hour. He knew this was their wedding anniversary and that Millicent was waiting for him with a little package. He shook his attaché case close by his ear to be sure his present was still there. He hesitated at the subway entrance and hurried on. J.C. was expecting him. He would be presiding over the big round table in the corner with a pitcher of martinis in his hand.

"I'll see you at the Happy Hour," he had said as they finished selecting art work for the Crown Thanksgiving ad.

David Copperton was a typically subservient man in

a gray flannel suit. He turned dutifully through the carved wooden door, knowing that this could be the breaking point of a marriage that was already bent by the sessions at the Happy Hour.

The first sentence in the last paragraph is superfluous authorial comment. David Copperton is proving the statement by thought and deed; it is not necessary to step out of his viewpoint to beat the reader over the head with it. Note the word "dutifully" in the following sentence. It is in the same category.

Such redundancy is not only out of viewpoint but it gilds the lily. It should be eliminated whether it occurs in single words, phrases, sentences, or paragraphs. Necessary author's comment should be converted to viewpoint whenever possible. The author's part in viewpoint is not on the printed page.

Another form of intrusion is more insidious; it creeps into virtually every writer's manuscript. It happens when the writer allows his personal opinions to override the viewpoint of his character and consequently warp the portrayal. Let's say we are writing about John J. Gotrocks III, who was born and bred to enjoy the better things in life. To date, he has had twenty-one years of practice:

John J. eased his car to a stop in front of the Yacht Club. By the time he got around to open the door for Bernice he had decided on the I-want-you-to-help-me-pick-a-gift-for-mother line. He watched the blonde's long legs unfold as she got out of the plush Cadillac. A fitting decoration for any man's apartment, if he could just get her there. John J. wondered if she had seen many etchings.

Everything in the above paragraph will pass viewpoint muster except for the word "plush" attached to John J.'s Cadillac. Anyone with as much money as John J. Gotrocks III takes a Cad for granted; he doesn't think of it as "plush" or "ritzy" or "expensive." Such thinking is out-of-character and, consequently, out-of-viewpoint.

Such descriptive words and phrases, which sneak into a story, represent the author's attitude but are alien to the character's viewpoint. They should be searched out and eliminated.

VII

TIME AND VIEWPOINT

———•◦•———

In fiction, Time exists as a paradox. For that reason its handling can become rather sticky. From back in the misty past when our ancestors hunkered around fires in smoky caves and regaled each other with grunted tales of derring-do, fictional narrative has been told in the past tense because it related events which occurred in the past. However, from the earliest grunt to the present, a dramatic narrative has had only one purpose: To tell of past events in such a way as to make the listener or reader live the story vicariously in a state of anxiety because of what is likely to happen to the viewpoint character in his future.

Most writers experiment with verb tense at one time or another, but in the long run, the past tense seems to do the most effective job of transporting the reader out of his world back into another. One of the writer's omnipresent problems is keeping his reader oriented in time while he is making the necessary tense manipulations unobtrusively as possible. If at any point your reader has to stop reading—or go back and reread—in order to find out where he is in time, you have lost him from the mainstream of your story.

To keep the reader within the web of his story, the writer must exercise maximum control over the reader's heart and mind while making transitions of time, place, and viewpoint.

Flashback

It would be a great convenience to the writer if he could thoroughly acquaint his reader with the backgrounds of the participating characters, the situation, and the time, place and social atmosphere before beginning his story. This is seldom practical, but if it is done at all, it must be executed with great finesse to be successful. As we said in a previous chapter, various forces have operated to make this approach more a part of the historical development of the art of story-telling than a technique to be applied by the modern writer. Writers are now constrained to limit their narration of the past only to those details which have a direct bearing on the drama at hand. This portion of a narrative has come to be called "flashback."

It will help us in dealing with the problems of flashback presentation to understand why we must limit ourselves to a minimum of the past. The reason deals a painful blow to nostalgia: *The past is of absolutely no dramatic value unless it poses a threat in the future.* This gives us a basis for judging the value of any flashback we are contemplating, as well as the key to selecting the best method of presentation. Fortunately, the proper use of viewpoint techniques can greatly help solve our problems.

Another point should be made regarding the dramatic value of the past: A past of which the viewpoint character has no prior knowledge and over which he has had no control is of dubious dramatic value, because it can serve neither to develop the character nor to contribute to emotional suspense. Let's look at an example which we might entitle "Bar Sinister":

Jonathan Witt is an executive in a large corporation which operates on a world-wide scale. Jonathan is called into the office of Winthrop Withers, the president, and informed that he is going to be assigned to take over the London office, which will now be responsible for the entire European complex. Jonathan is rather surprised, because he has never made a secret of his interest in the pleasures of life, and W.W. is so strait-laced that he insisted upon his daughter's fiancé being able to trace his ancestry to Puritan stock before he would consent to the marriage. However, Jonathan is jubilant; this represents a substantial promotion. Jonathan must have a passport to go to London. He fills out the necessary application, sends for his birth certificate, which he has never seen, and leaves the details to be attended to while he is on a business trip. The birth certificate arrives while he is away. W.W. sees it and learns that Jonathan's mother was not married at the time of his birth and that his father was listed as "unknown." W.W. says that the company cannot have a bastard filling a post of such responsibility. Jonathan will not head the London office.

As it stands, the above synopsis represents only an incident, an anecdote with an ironic twist; in no respect does it have the fiber necessary for drama. If there is going to be a real story, the events in it will follow in time what is synopsized above. Jonathan had no knowledge of his situation until the past, over which he had no control, was revealed to him. His future may be full of drama as a result, but up to this point his past could be of no dramatic value because there was no opportunity for it to evoke an emotional response within him.

Now let's alter the facts: Let's say that Jonathan knew of his origin. Knowing W.W.'s outlook on humanity, Jonathan certainly would not have informed him, and so his past could be a threat to his future. Let's add to his troubles: Jonathan's wife and children do not know of his past. However, his secretary does, and Jonathan has committed an indiscretion with her which may have left her with a scar. Also, his competitor for the London post, another executive, has employed a detective to delve into Jonathan's past. We now have a situation in which the past definitely poses a threat in the future. Jonathan Witt will be motivated by his past; he will be in emotional suspense. He will have to make decisions and take action because of it.

The presentation of flashback material is a bugaboo to most beginning writers. They are thinking of their story in terms of its on-stage action, but the past hangs over them as a necessary evil. Three possibilities usually occur: The Gob-Lot Method, The Hook-'Em-and-Tell-'em Technique, and The Shoehorn Squeeze. None of the three is desirable; consequently, you should be able to recognize the difficulties inherent in each, in case you are tempted:

The gob-lot method is based on the philosophy of getting the past out of the way in a hurry so one can get on with the story. The writer usually assembles all of his flashback material in a wad and attempts to shape it into an attractive beginning. More often than not, this doesn't work. It delays getting the principal character into the "now" of the story situation. Also, the compression tends to give the reader a confusing, undigestible mass of facts and information before he gets to know the people to whom they are related. In many cases, the real hero or heroine is either disguised or lost, with the result that the reader enters the story in a fog.

The hook'em-and-tell'-em technique is based on the common advice that the writer should begin his story at a high point. (There is nothing wrong with this advice.) However, having started his story at a high point, the writer believes his reader will be irretrievably hooked, and he is likely to bring his living narrative to a screaming stop with an awkward transition into a dead past as he reaches back into time to bring his reader up to date. This can lose the reader in the sequence of time and interrupt the emotional suspense. The sudden intrusion into the story's high point gives the reader a letdown, creating the impression that what is going on really isn't so important after all if it can be interrupted.

The shoehorn squeeze occurs when the writer begins by putting the "now" of his story on paper in its entirety and then goes back to insert the necessary flashback during rewriting. He usually searches out various points at which he can pry apart the narrative and squeeze in bits of the past. The result is somewhat comparable to Shakespearean players attempting to perform in front of an ineptly painted backdrop in an old-time vaudeville theater. The flashback has not been integrated into the story. It usually stands out, jarring the reader as badly as if he were being nudged by the writer's elbow.

As I said earlier, the proper use of viewpoint techniques will solve most of the writer's problems with flashback. When a story is written in viewpoint, it is logical for the principal character to think of the past at such times as that past is motivating him in the story present. Viewing the story from his viewpoint, the reader will simply learn of the past naturally, as it passes through the viewpoint character's mind. And better yet, the reader will experience the motivation and become aware of the future threat simultaneously with the character he is following.

Let's pick up Jonathan Witt's story and see how this works. The flashback is printed in italics for ready identification:

> As Jonathan headed back toward his office, he had to force himself to walk slowly enough to maintain the appearance of dignity. *The new London post had been so far beyond his wildest dreams that he had given it no thought. He hadn't even told Karen about it.* He wanted to get back to his office and think things out before he had to talk to anybody else. But his secretary obviously already knew.
>
> Janet was standing in the doorway with his attaché

case and a tightly rolled umbrella. A paper derby hat from *last year's Christmas party* was cocked over her eye.

"I say, old chap, that was a bit of all right! Wot!"

And then Jonathan realized that it had been in the back of his mind not to take Janet with him to London. *Things had been pretty awkward since the trip to Boston.*

"Congratulations, boss." Janet kissed him squarely on the lips. It was not a secretarial peck.

Damn it! How could you tell a woman she didn't own part of you after *you had told her you loved her?*

"Thanks, Janet. I-I appreciate the reception." He nodded toward the umbrella. "I guess— I guess I need to go in and pinch myself until I'm sure it's really true."

He ducked into the sanctuary of his private office. But he found no peace there. Karen was smiling at him out of the picture on the credenza behind his desk. Jonathan swore softly. Damn *champagne flights!* Why in the hell *had he let himself get drunk enough to go along with the gag and register as Mr. and Mrs. because a hotel clerk had made a stupid mistake?* Or had there been a mistake? *It had been Janet who made the reservations. And it had been she who suggested it.*

"Why not? We're just going to use it to dress for the banquet."

And then the snow storm came and Boston was socked in. The irony of it was that Karen had started the whole thing.

"One of us has to be here for Penny's recital or she will think she has done all of that practicing for nothing. Why don't you take Janet to that stupid old banquet or whatever it is in Boston?"

So he had taken Janet to Boston, with Karen trusting him every mile of the way. Damn! Jonathan turned away from Karen's picture. He felt dirty inside, sickish at his stomach. What a hell of a way to kick off the biggest thing that ever happened to him.

His buzzer gave two short beeps. The office door opened and Janet came in. She had a handful of papers.

"Mr. Withers told me last week, right after the board meeting, so I could be getting started on your passport." She shook the papers. *"I have already gotten the official copy of your birth certificate."*

She came around the desk and leaned over his shoulder. Too close. He could feel the warmth of her body. No woman should be allowed to wear perfume like that at ten o'clock in the morning.

"I suppose Karen and the children will go over after we do, what with the children being in school and all."

"Damn it, I'm not sure yet that you—"

The black and white photostat of the birth certificate caught his eye. Janet's long red fingernail was casually pointing to the blank that said, "FATHER'S NAME: *Unknown.*" She knew. Good God! Old Winthrop Withers would blow the whole thing sky-high if he ever found out that *he was a bastard,* and Janet darned well knew it, too. There wasn't much doubt that she would be going to London with him.

"I'm sorry I snapped at you." Jonathan put his hand over hers. "I—I guess this has all happened too suddenly."

He felt her lips on the back of his neck, soft and wet. "Darling, you're just a grumpy old keyed-up executive who needs to unwind." Her fingers caressed his cheek. "Maybe in Boston."

Jonathan felt pain slicing through his stomach and knew that his ulcer was going on another rampage.

Note that flashback occurs in the narrative only as it occurs to Jonathan's mind *in the living present of the story.* This is a reflection of the normal workings of the human mind. Something in the present triggers the mind to reach back into the past; the past then motivates the viewpoint character's thoughts, emotional reactions, and actions. Under such conditions, the past almost inevitably begins to loom as a threat in the future. So it becomes obvious that the viewpoint character is the ideal vehicle in a dramatic presentation for furnishing the reader with information about the past.

The writer should never take this as license to present flashback material to the reader "all in a piece," even though it might all be done in viewpoint. This is simply not how the human mind works. Our minds dance back and forth between the present and the past. Note that the present always occurs before the past; that is, the present provides one with the motivation to think about the past.

Nor is flashback realistically presented in straight narrative discourse. We do not sit around mentally telling ourselves how we react to our pasts in passionately purple prose, as did Tom Jones:

> It is difficult for any who have not felt it, to conceive the glowing warmth which filled his breast on the first contemplation of this victory over his passion. Pride flattered him so agreeably, that his mind perhaps enjoyed perfect happiness; but this was only momentary: Sophia soon returned to his imagination, and allayed the joy of his triumph with no less bitter pangs than a good-natured general must feel, when he surveys the bleeding heaps at the price of whose blood he hath purchased his laurels; for thousands of tender ideas lay murdered before our conqueror.

Actually our pasts drift through our minds in shapeless, unformed, and more often than not, uncontrolled patterns—all at lightning speed—which we simply cannot verbalize precisely. Attempts to reproduce the exact workings of the mind are generally called "stream of consciousness,"* and experimentation in this area has undoubtedly been responsible for considerable refinement in the use of viewpoint. One might say that the more nearly the writer approaches a stream-of-consciousness technique, the deeper he is in his character's viewpoint.

How deeply the writer can go into viewpoint—that is, how far he can go toward reproducing in the story the actual ramblings and incoherencies of the human mind —is dependent upon the writer's ability and the receptivity of his audience. Although there are obviously exceptions, as a generality it can be said that *deep* stream of consciousness is for the intellectually elite readers who derive their entertainment from esthetic appreciation or from ferreting out the meanings rather than participating in the drama or watching it take place.

The techniques of viewpoint and of stream of consciousness are the same; the difference is a matter of

* The phrase "stream of consciousness" was probably first used by William James, psychologist and philosopher. A less realistic form of the technique has been called "interior monologue." Edgar Allan Poe, Herman Melville, and Henry James were forerunners of the technique. James Joyce's *Ulysses* is probably most representative of true stream-of-consciousness style. Conrad Aiken, Sherwood Anderson, James T. Farrell, William Faulkner, Ernest Hemingway, John dos Passos, Gertrude Stein, W. C. Williams, Virginia Woolf, and Thomas Wolfe were followers of Joyce to various degrees. Eugene O'Neill's *Strange Interlude* was an attempt to apply stream-of-consciousness technique to drama.

degree. When the writer writes in a stream-of-consciousness style, he is immersing himself deeply in the character and attempting to reproduce the workings of the
subjective mind. When the writer is writing in viewpoint, he is creating an illusion of the reality of the
human mind. His character's thinking, his mental delv-
ing into the past and contemplating the present and
future is flavored with the individual's habit of thought
and vernacular. However, the writer exercises selective
control over what he allows to occur in his character's
mind so that there will be no lapse in the emotional
state in which he has suspended his reader.

In the Jonathan Witt story, note the fairly long section of flashback which furnished the reader with information concerning the association between Jonathan
and Janet in Boston: It starts with Jonathan being motivated to think about the past by his wife's picture;
then the verb tense shifts to the past perfect (the "had"
form) to signal to the reader that he is being transported
back into time (". . . *had* he *let* himself . . . a clerk
had made . . . It *had been* Janet. . . . And it *had
been* she who . . ."). When Jonathan's mind comes
back out of the past, the transition is made on the same
motivation; he is still looking at Karen's picture. He
turns away from the picture, and the tense changes from
the past perfect to the past. The reader thus knows that
he is back in the present of the story.

The use of this flashback entry and exit technique—
of going into and coming out of flashback on the same
motivation—allows the writer to communicate without
having to nudge the reader with such obvious verbal

signposts as, "A few months ago in Boston. . . . He brought his mind back to the present." In addition, this device is a realistic reflection of the way in which we are reminded to think of things in the past and the way in which our minds return to the present world immediately about us.

If a flashback scene is long, it is sometimes advisable to orient the reader in time by use of the past perfect tense and then shift back to the simple past. This avoids the rhetorical awkwardness of so many "had" verb forms, and it tends to bring the scene closer to the reader. Then, when coming out of flashback, return to the past perfect tense before coming back into the story present via the past tense. For example:

> Jonathan watched Tim square away at the plate and wave his bat at the pitcher. He felt Karen go tense, and he put his hand over hers.
>
> "Make him hit it!" yelled the shortstop. "Old Timmy boy's gonna hit to me."
>
> Jonathan remembered that things had been different when he played baseball, painfully different. Like the championship playoff—two out, bases loaded, last of the ninth, and they were one run behind.
>
> "Pitch to me, boy, pitch to me. This bastard's an easy out."
>
> The plate umpire was from the South Side. He didn't know Jonathan. He objected to the catcher's language.
>
> "Sir, I beg to differ with you. I was not cursing. I was stating a fact." The boy was meticulously polite. "You ask anybody on the North Side, and he'll tell you Jonathan Witt's father was not married to his mother. And, sir, I believe that is the definition of *bastard*. Isn't that right, Jonathan?"

The umpire looked at him, red-faced, his mouth hanging open. Finally he mumbled his way back to crouch behind the catcher. Jonathan had watched three strikes whiz across the plate and thunk into the glove of the snickering catcher. The coach had—

The bat cracked, and Jonathan stood along with everybody else to watch Tim round first and slide into second, hooking the bag with his foot and writhing away from the second baseman's stabbing glove.

" 'At'sa way, Timmy boy!"

Jonathan sat back down as the others sat down. Children were like that, cruel. He could never subject his son to having some snot-nosed catcher greet him at the plate with "Say, Witt, didn't I hear your old man's a bastard?" He turned to Karen.

"I-I've got to make a phone call. I'll go to that booth down behind the bleachers."

He couldn't fight it. He would call Janet and tell her that she was going to London with him. She had been right; he couldn't get along without her.

As a sidelight, note that the use of viewpoint keeps the writer from having to *tell* the reader. Granted that the reader was pretty thoroughly in viewpoint and sympathetic to Jonathan by the time he came to the above story quote, it would not be necessary for the writer to indicate the viewpoint character's emotional reaction. Each reader would feel it in a way that would be plausible to him; therefore, he would understand the decision which is taking place within the character's mind.

The past is often such a strong factor in motivating a change in a character's emotional state in the story present that it can appear to the writer that the change actually took place during the flashback. The writer's tendency is to bring the character out of the flashback in the new emotional state which resulted from the motivation of the past. This is not effective. *Always show your character's emotional reactions and his decisions in the living present of the story.*

All of this is not to say that flashback is always presented from within the viewpoint character's mind; for example, note Janet's explanation of how it happened that she knew about Jonathan's appointment to the London office. It is often necessary to have information of the past come from some source other than the viewpoint character in order to maintain the logic of a single viewpoint character who could not have had access to the information.

An exchange of dialogue in which two or more characters recount the past can have the effect of making the flashback a direct part of the story present with consequent motivation taking place within the viewpoint character's mind. Many a good mystery thriller is nothing more than the trials and tribulations encountered by the principal character as he attempts to piece together past events by means of information gained from others.

One method of flashback presentation frequently attempted by inexperienced writers is the dream sequence. The result is inherently weak in its impact and more often than not highly contrived in its effect. Although much of our actual contemplation of the past is a sort of daydreaming process and we are often motivated to thought, feeling, and action as a result, seldom do we even remember enough of our night-time mental meanderings for them to serve as stimuli. Take a strong sleeping potion any time you are tempted to have a fictional dream.

Transitions

The writer's problem would be greatly simplified if he could tell his story from beginning to end as one continuous narrative, proceeding in perfect chronological sequence, confined to a single viewpoint and to one place. However, this is almost never the case.

The writer must weave back and forth in time, now presenting flashback, now living in the story present, and then skipping dull passages of his viewpoint character's life. He must go from one place to another with his viewpoint character, and he will find occasions when he will have to transfer from one viewpoint character to another. In other words, he must make transitions in time, place, and viewpoint, and he must make them in such a way that the reader will be constantly oriented but will not be jarred out of the emotional suspense of the story by the mechanics of the orientation process.

Because time and space are universal factors in daily existence, they provide the writer with a prime tool for achieving reader identification and plausibility. In real life, we are constantly aware of not having time enough to do something, of not being in the right place at the right time, of the time it takes us to get from place to place. . . . Having your viewpoint character encounter one of those obstacles sets a responsive chord to twanging within your reader because this is a reflection of his own daily life. Transitions of time and place should always be made in viewpoint for maximum reader identification.

We have discussed how to present flashback material, which is essentially a problem of getting about in time. However, this is not the only variety of time transition which the writer must make. Many a segment of your viewpoint character's life needs to be skipped because it is not relevant to the main stream of your drama. As offstage action it will provide necessary narrative continuity or lend plausibility without slowing the progress of your story or diminishing its emotional impact.

The problem is twofold: Keep your reader aware of the passage of time; and, in the process, maintain his identification with the viewpoint character's problem. This is best accomplished by clearly erecting time markers and road signs on both sides of the missing slice of time and giving emphasis to the character's emotional state, also on both sides of the transition, thus making the reader aware that the viewpoint character, his problem, and the resulting emotional state have all crossed the missing segment of the calendar. For example:

John Williston began surveying the beach at Sombolique at eight o'clock on Monday morning as he had for the past four days: Literally acres of tender flesh, covered by the scantiest of bikinis and studded with sunglasses, stretched before him. For five long years John had deprived himself of the better things in life to get to Sombolique, "the best place in the world to meet a woman with money."

In his mind's eye, he counted and recounted the traveler's checks, but there were only ten left. In spite of the glaring sun and the overtone of warmth radiating from the generous display of feminine flesh, a cold chill passed over John's body, brought on by the misty perspiration of panic. He had so little time in which to learn how a man could tell if a woman had money when she wore only sunglasses and a bikini.

By Friday morning, the supply of traveler's checks had dwindled to three, and the panic was turning to sweating fear. John had spent one check learning that the beautifully adorned blonde in the hot pink bikini had smiled at him because she was at Sombolique for the same purpose as he. He invested another precious five hundred francs to learn that the most beautiful tan on the beach could be acquired by a waitress from one of the hotels.

A line of white space is used in the above example to indicate to the reader that the narrative has skipped a stretch of time. You may or may not need to use white space as a signal. If a short period of time is involved and the reader is adequately oriented, the white space is really unnecessary. The writer has only to be sure that he is putting as much on paper as he knows; in other words, a transition may be perfectly obvious to the writer but obscure to the reader.

It is worth noting that what takes place during a transition—in other words, what is missing in the white space—can often be more vivid to the reader than if it were described in detail. The reader uses his own imagination to supply the details. Let's take sexual activities, for example. When intimate details are supplied, the identification of individual readers is often lost for any one of several reasons: The details may not agree with the reader's personal experience: the reader's basic morals may be violated, the reader's sense of decency may be breached, etc.—the effect of which shocks the reader out of viewpoint. However, if the reader has been sympathetically identified with the viewpoint character up to the beginning of a transition in time and the details of the activities are not supplied, the reader can project himself into the situation as he would perform or as he would see it. He will come out on the other side of the transition still in viewpoint, as a result of having participated in a scene which was actually not on the paper before him.

The writer often tends to overlook the measurement of time by making reference to vague spans, such as "A few days later . . . several years before . . . in a few weeks . . ." The use of precise times is much more effective: "Ten minutes before . . . the next morning . . . on Friday at eight o'clock . . ." This may require the writer to prepare a time table for his narrative, particularly for a long work, but the process of doing so will eliminate many a chance for implausibility or incredibility.

Note that in the above example—a transition of *time* without a change of *place*—the transition is measured in both time and money. The traveler's checks act as a "road sign" of sorts, comparable to going into and out of flashback. The reader is not only kept aware of the passage of time, but he is oriented to the urgency of the viewpoint character's problem by way of his dwindling funds.

A transition of place always involves a transition of time, because time is an inevitable factor in getting from place to place—as every reader who has been in a hurry knows. The writer must erect road signs and mileposts for his viewpoint character to see so the reader can tell where he is in time and space. For example:

> Will Epperson swung his pony in a wide loop to nudge a recalcitrant mossyhorn back into the stream of cattle he was nursing up the Chisholm Trail. It took considerable dodging and chousing and enough names to peel a Gila monster before the steer would admit who was top hand. Will would have been glad for the diversion if the slashing ill-tempered beast hadn't somehow reminded him of Sledge Martin.
>
> The trembling, sinking feeling in his belly told Will that he was still afraid of Sledge. And Sledge would be waiting for him in Abilene, cold-eyed and angry.
>
> A hundred and seventy dusty miles and fourteen days of thinking brought Will no closer to courage. He could see Abilene on the horizon, even through the column of dust that hung over the herd. Abilene and Sledge Martin. Will could feel damp coldness in the palms of his hands. Slowly he unfastened his gun belt, rolled it around his holstered six-gun, and stowed it in his saddlebag. Will shook his head. As his father would have said, that was a hell of a place for a man to carry his guts.

Not only do you need to let your reader know where your viewpoint character is going and how long it is taking him to get there, but you need to emphasize your character's emotional state so that your reader will know that the drama's real reason for being has survived the trip. This information does not come to the reader as a concrete realization; he knows only that he wants to keep on reading. The story is sustaining his interest.

On occasion, there may be the necessity for a change in the character's emotional state during a transition of time and/or space. Let's say that during the fourteen days it took for Will Epperson to get to Abilene, he screwed up his courage by mental communication with his father. By the time he got to Abilene, he had lost his fear and was ready to face Sledge Martin. However, the change was so gradual and the accompanying events were so bland that the period did not deserve the spotlight of shared participation on the part of the character and the reader during the entire sequence. In other words, even though the principal character changed during the time span, it was a relatively dull section which would better be bridged by a transition.

In such a case, *do not let your character arrive at the end of a transition in a different emotional state, even though the change occurred during the transition.* Take your character across the missing time span in the "old" emotional state. Then show the change by way of flashback in his viewpoint. Let's pick up Will Epperson just before he arrives in Abilene:

> The trembling, sinking feeling in his belly told Will that he was still afraid of Sledge. And Sledge would be waiting for him in Abilene, cold-eyed and angry.

> The fear of Sledge Martin simmered and boiled within Will Epperson during most of the fourteen days it took to prod the herd through the Indian nations along a hundred and seventy miles of dusty trail. He

began to dread the nights when he could hear his father's voice booming at him above the murmur of the gently stirring cattle, "If a man don't have guts enough to die, he's already dead. . . . The only time to run is when you're wrong. When you're right, fight for it."

By the time he could see Abilene, hanging hazy on the horizon through the column of dust that welled up from the herd, Will knew that he was right and that he wasn't going to run—from Sledge Martin or anybody else. He took his gun belt out of his saddlebag and strapped it about his middle. The cold wet left the palms of his hands.

As an aside, when making transitions of place, research your travel times. It doesn't take much effort to find out that trail herds were taken up the old Chisholm Trail at speeds ranging from ten to twenty miles a day with twelve miles as an average toward the end of the drive. If you are writing Westerns, a lot of your readers will know this; so should you.

Recently I edited a piece in which a couple covered 160 kilometers (100 miles) in a "leisurely two-hour drive" on the tortuous, town-infested, traffic-clogged stretch of road along the Rhine River. In actuality, a driver would have to have one foot on the accelerator, the other on the brake, and his nose to the steering wheel to average thirty kilometers an hour. The plausibility of the story would be destroyed for a reader who knew the facts.

The author had previously made the trip on a river steamer. His research had consisted of checking the distance between two points in a road atlas. To him, a resident of Arizona, fifty miles per hour was a leisurely drive in the wide-open spaces surrounding his home.

Changing emotions

A dramatic story could be defined in terms of an emotional plot line, that is, as a progression of emotional states in the viewpoint character, which result from the various stimuli to which he is subjected. Admittedly, such a definition is spurious in that it emphasizes the means rather than the end. It is somewhat comparable to dismissing Michelangelo's Pietà as two figures carved from marble. However, stress on the story's emotional line points up a reality which the writer must face.

Basically, the writer achieves impact by communicating his viewpoint character's emotional state to his reader. This communication is comparable to the transmission of automotive power from the motor to the wheels: There is inevitable loss. The writer must compensate for this loss.

A major reason for the loss of emotional thrust between the writer and the reader can be traced to the very thing which generates the drama, the writer's feeling for his materials. Since the writer's story is erupting onto paper out of his own feelings, he is prone to assume that the reader will feel as he does, simply because he (the writer) is so moved by his story in the process of living it onto paper. Let's look at part of a story as it might appear in the writer's working synopsis:

. . . It was the last straw when Carleton compared Melanie to one of the cheap women he had met in New

Orleans. Since that night she locks her bedroom door. She spends the long winter nights in her lonely bed, penetrating in a thousand ways the veneer of gentility which makes her the most envied woman in Natchez.

Every night Carleton tries the door and then says, "I'm going out, Melanie dear. Don't wait up." And she would hear the clopping of his horse as he rode away to one of the riverfront brothels. "With a little more paint and a little more wiggle, you'd be as good as Big Nose Nelly" reverberates through her mind. Through a hundred long nights, revulsion grows to hate.

Then spring comes. One evening, through an open window, she watches little Betsy playing with her doll. Melanie remembers her own childhood and how much she had wanted a baby sister. That night she left her bedroom door unlocked. . . .

Obviously, one strong emotional state is overpowering another strong emotional state. By the time spring comes, neither Melanie nor the reader is going to think much of Carleton. Then, as a progression of the plot, Melanie's emotional state must change; her desire for motherhood must be awakened, motivated by her reaction to seeing a little girl playing with a doll.

As the story is conceived and grows in the writer's mind, this motivation takes place within the writer and leads to whatever will be the results of Melanie's leaving her bedroom door unlocked. In the process of putting the story on paper and moving it on to the next big scene, the writer is likely to gloss over the changes of emotions in the viewpoint character. This will result in a serious loss of reader impact, no matter how big the next scene may be.

For example, let's say Melanie merely opens her door to another insult from Carleton. If the writer has been successful in communicating the strength of Melanie's desire for motherhood to the reader, the reader will sympathize with her. If the writer has not been successful, the reader is likely to think that Melanie got what she deserved for being so stupid and from then on lose interest in what happens to her.

The writer must remember that after building a strong emotional state in the viewpoint character as a result of powerful emotion, he will have to create equally strong or even stronger motivation to change plausibly that emotional state in *both* character and reader. This necessity is merely a reflection of life. When we are worked up to a high pitch, it takes time and motivation to change us; we do not flit lightly from one intense emotional state to another, even if we want to do so.

Changing viewpoint

Without question, single-viewpoint narration is the most successful means of sustaining the reader's interest in a story. Any time a writer shifts from the viewpoint of one character to the viewpoint of another, he runs the risk of losing a substantial portion of any vicarious participation and interest he has built up within the reader to that point. This is particularly true if the outlook of the second viewpoint character is substantially different from the outlook of the first.

However, there comes a time in every writer's life when he must leave the viewpoint of the Lone Ranger and switch over to riding with Tonto, the Lone Ranger's faithful Indian companion. There are certain techniques which will make the transition less risky.

Above all, the reader must never be confused as to whose viewpoint he is in. Emphasize viewpoint both before and after the change. Immediately at the beginning of narration in the new viewpoint get inside of the character's mind and body; at this point avoid any purely descriptive material or objective narration which will not help orient the reader.

Again put up "signs" so that it will be clear to the reader that he is in a new viewpoint and indicate what character he is "living with." One particularly useful technique is to have the new viewpoint character see the old one immediately after the transition. For example:

> Charley Weeks fought the freeway traffic all the way to Rocheport. It seemed worse than ever tonight because he was so anxious to get home on account of the trouble with Junior. He braked for the exit and snatched the new .22 rifle to keep it from sliding off the seat. The burled stock was silky in his hand, and he fondled it for a moment before giving his full attention to the steering wheel. What wouldn't he have given for a rifle like that when he was a kid!
>
> The rifle had better do the job. Charley hated to admit it, but he was at the end of his rope. No matter what the psychiatrist said, he couldn't hold out against Louise any longer. He wheeled into the driveway, grabbed the rifle, and headed for the house. He carried the rifle behind him in case Junior happened to be looking; Charley wanted to see his face when he saw the rifle for the first time. Louise was waiting.
>
> "Now, Charles, I don't care what Dr. Schmitt says,

we are going right out and get him a BB gun. Six days of locking himself alone in his room without eating is just too much. And, Charles, I called around and most of the other boys do have—"

Louise stopped talking as Charley brought the rifle from behind his back.

"Just cast your peepers on what I got him. It's a ring-tailed honey!"

As the new rifle glistened in the light, Charley felt a glow coursing through him. He snuggled it to his shoulder, and the stock caressed his cheek like warm flesh as he sighted along the blue octagonal barrel. Oh boy! Wait'll he sees it!

Charley took the stairs two at a time and rapped on Junior's door. "Hey, Juney! It's me—your dad."

" 'Djya get my BB gun?" Junior's voice was faint against the background of a throbbing transistor radio.

"Wait'll you see it! Open up."

The lock rattled and the door inched open. Charley pushed into the midst of the sound, holding the rifle behind his back. Junior turned off the transistor and craned. Charley thrust the rifle out between them. Junior was ringed with colored lights through the tears that were filming Charley's eyes.

"I got two boxes of cartridges. First thing in the morning we'll go out and I'll teach you how to really shoot with this baby."

Junior saw the heavy blue octagonal barrel lying in his father's hand. Cripes, a .22! The hope drained away, leaving only the gnawing hunger in his stomach, and Junior was afraid he was going to cry.

The old man had blown it again. All he wanted was a BB gun so he could go down to the dump and pop at tin cans and bottles with the fellows. His father would never let him take the rifle alone. He looked down at the radio in his hand to hide the tingling tears.

"I wanna BB gun." Junior turned the transistor to full volume and sat down on the floor.

It will further help orient the reader and sharpen the characterization, if the narrative styles of the two viewpoints are sufficiently different for the reader to distinguish between them, even without character identification. Each character should have an individualistic thought and speech pattern which is reflected in narration through his viewpoint. These patterns should be accented before and after the viewpoint transition. The change of viewpoint may or may not be emphasized by extra white space, depending upon the nature of the transition. Neither the use of distinctive narrative patterns nor the use of white space obviates the necessity for verbally orienting the reader.

Note in the above example that most of the wordage is spent in Charley's viewpoint, and Junior seems like pretty much of a brat with his hunger strike and his music and with the psychiatrist against him. In spite of Charley's faintly discernible ulterior motive in buying the rifle for Junior, there is sympathy for him as a beleaguered parent. But after a few words in Junior's viewpoint, Charley becomes an overindulgent parent who should have known better. From this point on, the reader would have to have an inherent sympathy for one side or the other for there to be substantial reader identification.

The potential loss in dramatic impact from the use of multiple viewpoint is so great that the writer should examine every possibility of narrating a story in a single viewpoint before committing himself to a plot which requires changes in viewpoint. The writer should never use viewpoint transition merely as a convenient method of transmitting information to the reader. Before the writer decides to use multiple viewpoint he must be convinced that the material of the story demands it.

VIII

DIALOGUE AND VIEWPOINT

———•••———

Like Caesar's Gaul, all dialogue is divided into three parts: One part consists of the actual *spoken words;* another the *identification of the speaker;* and the third is *stage business* or descriptive action, or how the speaker speaks and what he is doing while he talks. The arrangement and relationship of these parts and their content are controlled in one way or another by viewpoint.

Viewpoint provides the seat in the theater, the position from which the participants in the drama are heard and seen. The prose writer who is writing in viewpoint has a distinct advantage over the dramatist. The fiction writer can put his readers within the very heart of the story he is telling, inside the living, feeling, being of one of his story characters. Everything else in the story scene must be heard and seen from the viewpoint position from which it logically derives. Otherwise the dialogue will be faulty, and the writer will not communicate his meaning to the reader in a natural, uninterrupted flow.

If at any time the reader has to stop to search for the

writer's meaning, the writer has lost reader impact, since he has allowed the reader to escape from his story. Any time the mechanics of the narration stand out above the drama of the story, the reader's participation in the story's emotional impact and meaning is interrupted. This can happen in any aspect of fiction writing, but most often in dialogue.

The total effect of dialogue must be achieved by a blending of its three component parts. However, we can best approach the techniques of dialogue by analyzing each of the three parts, even though there will of necessity be some overlapping.

The spoken word

"How much dialogue should I have?" is a perennial question of beginning writers. They are usually referring to the actual spoken words which are normally surrounded by quotation marks in the text. There can be no positive answer to this question. It not only depends on the individual writer's facility with dialogue, but also on the writer's inner approach to the creation of his story: Does he primarily hear his story as it is performed by the actors within his mind? Does he mainly see it as people moving about within their environments in accordance with their relationships with one another? Or does his story just happen, with people within his heart creating their lives as an emotional experience within him?

Of course, there is probably a bit of each approach in all of us, but for each of us there is a definite slant toward one of those three creative bents. This bent controls our narrative style and, consequently, the amount of dialogue that we use in our stories. A story needs *precisely* as much dialogue as the writer requires to tell that story as he hears it and sees it and feels it. The word "precisely" is used to avoid any implication that this is a license for the wholesale use of quotation marks. The amount of dialogue the writer should use is determined by—and should be limited to—how much the story needs to express the writer's individual style and his particular story viewpoint. If there is one word of dialogue which is not required to characterize the actors and/or portray their participation in the drama which makes the story, that word has no place in the text.

The spoken word is by far the most expensive form of writing in terms of "spending" words. In addition to the words of the speaker, speaker identification and stage business (the other two components of dialogue) are necessary to give the depth to dramatic narrative which makes it possible for the reader to project himself into the story. To illustrate these points, let us take a short passage containing a normal blend of narration, exposition, description, and dialogue, and convert this to *all* dialogue, with a minimum of speaker identification. First the passage:

Arm-in-arm with Richard, Natalie walked into the library. The diamonds in her new ring sparkled as the chandelier came to blazing life. It was their library now. The warm brown booky view was briefly tarnished as Natalie remembered that a library was something her father had always wanted, but he died too soon. She felt Richard's hand guiding her. She found herself facing the fireplace, glowing with its cheery, crackling fire.

But she couldn't look at it. A beady-eyed woman staring at her out of the portrait above the mantel commanded her to look up. Natalie shivered and found herself clutching Richard's arm. Ridiculous! Who ever heard of being afraid of an oil painting? One thing was sure: That dour old biddy would have to go! Richard made a sweeping gesture toward the portrait.

"Isn't mother wonderfully regal? She'll be here first thing in the morning."

And now, let's try an "all dialogue" version of the same passage:

"Richard, I like for you to hold my arm as we walk."

"Natalie, I'll always be holding your arm, wherever we go together. And now I want to take you in to see the library."

"It's *our* library now, Richard."

"That it jolly well is! It's you and I to—"

"Richard! The light— It's so bright."

"Honey, we need a bright light today, just so I can see the sparkle of the diamonds in your new ring and know you're mine."

"All because of that great big chandelier that you turned on. *Ooh!* So many books, and all brown."

"No matter how much you light this place, it is still going to be sort of brown all over. Brown is mother's favorite color. She has everything bound in brown."

"Brown is a warm color, Richard. It makes it look nice and warm in here. I remember my father liked books so much. He always wanted a library, but he died before we had money enough to get it."

"Now, Natalie, we are going to have none of this

sadness on our wedding day. I had a nice big fire built in the fireplace, just for you."

"Richard, you lead me around just as if we were dancing."

"I'd like nothing better than to dance through life with you."

"You do the leading; I'll follow."

"We're off to the end of the world."

"Oh, look at the fireplace. Richard, the fire is so cheery. It pops and crackles so loud, as if it were laughing."

"Well, why don't you look at it then? Why are you looking up there?"

"Richard, I just can't keep from looking at that woman in that picture over the fireplace."

"It's an oil painting."

"Her eyes! Richard, they look like little old beads, the way she is staring down at me out of that picture."

"Natalie, your hands feel cold! You are shivering. You are hanging on to me like you are afraid."

"Ridiculous! What is there to be afraid of?"

"You act as if you are afraid of that painting, Natalie."

To herself, Natalie thought, "I am, but I can't tell him! One thing is for sure: That dour old biddy will have to go!"

Aloud, Natalie said, "Why are you making with that grandiloquent point at the painted old girl above the mantel?"

"Isn't mother wonderfully regal? She'll be here first thing in the morning."

All right, so you don't like that version. Why don't you have a go at it? I can guarantee that in the process of trying to write such a passage entirely in dialogue you will learn a lot about the trials and tribulations of the spoken word. That "all dialogue" version took 398 words, in contrast with the 146 in the original passage; and it doesn't approach the success in communicating either the same facts or the same feeling. It is completely lacking in power to achieve reader identification.

The original was from within Natalie's mind. Try as you will, by the use of "pure" dialogue you cannot reach the reader with the same nuances of meaning that you can obtain by an admixture of all forms of prose discourse *and* the use of viewpoint to give the reader access to dramatic motivation and an understanding of the character. This points up how much the actors and the scenery contribute to the effect of drama in the visual media.

The spoken word can characterize, it can give information, it can develop conflict between individuals, it can move the plot, it can give reality to a scene—but without outside help, or unrealistic soliloquies, it cannot take the reader deep inside a character where the true seed of drama is rooted.

Speaker identification

Ideally, every character's speech pattern should be so distinctively his that no other identification of the speaker would be necessary. However, the exclusion of all other speaker identification is rarely possible or practical, and much of the time the writer has to let the reader know who uttered the speech which is within quotation marks.

Any time the speakers in a scene are not adequately identified, the reader has to walk his fingers up the page to the last name that was mentioned. When he sets out on this annoying journey, the reader is leaving the story. The writer has let him get away.

Unless there is another method of identification available as a natural development of the narrative, there is nothing to beat plain old "he said . . . she said . . . John said . . . Mary said." Beginning writers usually feel that the repetition of "said" is poor style. The word juts up out of their copy as they read it, aloud or to themselves. Their initial curative measure is usually to start reaching for synonyms for "said." This produces such passages as:

> "Mary, I can't find any clean shirts," John complained.
> "Maybe you could if you'd buy me a washing machine," Mary insinuated.
> "Let's not start that again," John warned.
> "John, I've never stopped," Mary asserted.
> "You can say that again," John bleated.
> "All right, I will: *I've never stopped!*" Mary screamed.
> "Where did you hide my pistol?" John demanded.

In actuality, during the reading process, a reader pays about as much attention to "said" as he does to a comma, a period, or some other punctuation mark. It serves as a how-to-read signal, just as do punctuation marks. If the writer has to nudge the reader by telling him that a speech is a warning or an insinuation, the dialogue is not sufficiently well written. The speech itself should express the warning or insinuation and even the manner in which it is spoken, thus obviating the necessity for the writer to attach a label.

The above exchange between Mary and John is grossly overwritten. The initial speech in the exchange identifies one of the speakers by using her name in direct address and the other by giving his name in a tag. The subsequent dialogue is not sufficiently involved for the reader to get lost. Let's try it again:

> "Mary, I can't find any clean shirts," John said.
> "Maybe you could if you'd buy me a washing machine."
> "Let's not start that again."
> "John, I've never stopped."
> "You can say that again!"
> "All right, I will: *I've never stopped!*"
> "Where did you hide my pistol?"

Strictly speaking, when writing is in viewpoint, the narrative—dialogue and all—strains through the viewpoint character's mind. When we hear someone talking to us utter an insinuation, it does not register in our minds as "he insinuated." We *do* react mentally, perhaps with an unspoken thought, "That was a nasty crack." It is that mental reaction which motivates our reply or action.

Without intimate knowledge of the viewpoint character's mental reaction, the reader may completely miss the point of a dialogue exchange, even though the meaning is firm in the writer's mind. For example, suppose our viewpoint character is a boy who is talking to his mother:

> Toby heard the rattling of the front door. That would be Dad. "Mother, I've got to start studying." He reached over and turned on the transistor.

"Toby, I just don't understand how you can stand to listen to that awful old music all evening long."

"Just habit, I guess." Toby turned off the radio. "This way I can hear you and Dad better."

That's what Toby and his mother said and what Toby heard and did. But let's rewrite the passage and see what the writer might have been trying to convey:

Toby heard the rattling of the front door. That would be Dad. "Mother, I've got to start studying." He reached over and turned on the transistor.

"Toby, I just don't understand how you can stand to listen to that awful old music all evening long."

No, she didn't understand. If she just knew, that awful old music was a lot better than hearing her and Dad yell at each other about why Dad wouldn't go to church. He wished God was dead so they wouldn't fight about Him so much.

"Just habit I guess." Toby turned off the radio. "This way I can hear you and Dad better."

Stage business

The combination of viewpoint and stage business or described action of the characters speaking provides a "living" position from which dialogue is heard and, consequently, gives perspective and sound to the scene. It shows the speakers and thus gives movement and life. It allows the reader to participate through the consciousness of a listener and to understand his reactions. It allows the writer to abbreviate or paraphrase a dull conversational exchange within the mind of the viewpoint character and reserve quotation marks for the most meaningful speeches. Additionally, it can identify speakers, making it unnecessary to add speech tags.

To write effective dialogue, the writer must spend a considerable amount of time observing speakers and noting his own mental and physical reactions during conversation. Most beginners write horribly stilted and unrealistic dialogue, simply because they have never really paid close attention to themselves and to others. When we converse, we express ourselves in grunts and shrugs and nods; we accompany our speech by smiling and frowning and pointing and squirming and drinking coffee and what-have-you. Our speech comes out in incomplete sentences and long sentences and short sentences and one- or two-word phrases. Information passes slowly and painfully and often incorrectly between people.

If you record a few actual exchanges of dialogue and then transcribe them, you will quickly prove to yourself that the writer cannot be absolutely realistic in writing dialogue—not if he wants readers. The result would be long, repetitious speeches. Most readers would drift away from the narrative from the sheer boredom of reading so much to get so little. Well-written dialogue creates an illusion of reality. The dialogue reads as if it were real, but the ramblings and incoherencies are held to the minimum necessary to create the illusion.

Seldom do you participate in an exchange of conversation during which you answer without prior mental, and many times emotional, reaction to the speech you have just heard. This would also be impossible to reproduce faithfully. The human mind is so incredibly

rapid in its processes that if the *total* stream of consciousness of the viewpoint character were reproduced,
the reader would forget what the speakers said from
speech to speech, while reading the interspersed goings-
on within the viewpoint character's mind. The desired
effect, therefore, must be created by an illusion of reality. It is part of the stage business of dialogue. During
a conversation, we notice the speaker's facial expressions and his movements, and also see and hear what is
going on around us. Again, because of the rapidity of
thought processes and the fact that most of what is going on is not relevant to a story, the writer must turn
reality into an illusion of reality to make it seem real.

The key to creating good realistic dialogue is the selection of what is *significant from the viewpoint position of the narrative:* The significant speeches, the significant reactions and thoughts of the viewpoint character, the significant effect of the viewpoint character
upon others, the significant actions and expressions of
characters other than the viewpoint, the significant
sounds of voices, the significant external objects and
happenings. Any word in your dialogue which cannot
stand the searching spotlight of that word "significant"
should go under the blue pencil.

When an exchange of dialogue appears in your final
manuscript, that exchange must be presented in a manner which will stand up logically from the viewpoint
position of the narrative. Here is a horrible example of
one of the most common mistakes (the offending portion is italicized):

Penelope's lips had disappeared into that thin black line. Marvin knew it was too late for explanations, but he had to try for peace before the deer season opened.

"Penny, I did everything I could to make your mother happy."

Her voice rasped out at him. "Like making up her bed with the dog's blanket and then fixing the bedroom door so it wouldn't latch?"

From a standpoint of logic, it is impossible for Marvin or anybody else to tell that Penelope's voice rasped before she spoke. She might have shook her fist, stomped, stuck out her tongue, or something else; but her voice could not be heard before she spoke. Any quotation introduced by a description of how the speech is going to sound is out. Sound which has not yet been heard cannot be described.

Stage business is most effectively placed at those points where it would naturally occur, which also happens to be where it will interfere least with the meaning and intonation of the spoken word. Again, a horrible example involving the ubiquitous cigarette:

"Penny, you've just got," *Marvin mashed his cigarette into the ashtray,* "to believe that was an accident. I didn't try to kill her. I simply didn't know she couldn't swim."

No one would mash his cigarette into an ashtray between "got" and "to" unless it was burning his fingers. Between the two sentences, yes. Place your stage business where there is a natural pause in the speech, where a pause would actually occur in a real conversation. You can make stage business serve both as a form of punctuation to help pace the reader's reading and to give emphasis to appropriate parts of a speech.

When your stage business serves to identify the speaker, labeling the speaker is unnecessary. For example:

> "Mother does try to get along with you. She—"
> Marvin pointed to the liquor cabinet. "Like when she poured that bottle of my good bourbon in the sink," *he said.*
> "She didn't know," *Penelope said, a tiny smirk starting at the corner of her mouth.* "She thought the decanter was a bud vase."

"He said" does absolutely nothing but take up space, since it is obvious that he said it. "Penelope said" is equally unnecessary. The stage business would identify the speaker without the label: "A tiny smirk started at the corner of Penelope's mouth."

If you always remember that your position as the writer is within the viewpoint character and that in your position the imaginary world in which you are the principal actor revolves about you, the communicative power of your dialogue will improve tremendously and many a heretofore sticky problem will work itself out more easily.

IX

BACKGROUND AND VIEWPOINT

———•••———

There was a time when the writer would almost invariably begin his story by establishing the background and setting of his narrative. He would describe in the minutest detail everything within the ken of the first character to be introduced. This was repeated for every change of scene. Such descriptions appeared in large blocks of type with few paragraph indentations to vary the monotony.

This method of handling background was convenient for the writer. He could completely establish the scene in which his character was going to act and then proceed with the action, confident that his reader would be thoroughly oriented. The confidence was misplaced.

The reluctant student of literature developed a reading technique which was soon adopted by the rank and file of readers: When he came to a large, solid block of dull gray type, he would skip with a scanning eye until he found the name of a character. If the meaning from then on was not clear, he could always go back and pick up loose ends. Teachers of literature tried to force more thorough reading by asking such penetrating questions as "What color were the curtains in Lord Balclutha's sitting room at the time of Lady Tenderly's first visit?" The reading technique worked well enough for the practical purposes of the casual academic. Reading for fun was another matter; this could be pretty deadly with what was available.

With the continual development of improved writing techniques, particularly in the viewpoint area, writers became more and more selective in the descriptive details which they included, and readers became more and more selective in their choice of reading material. The result has wrought considerable improvement in the art of communication. It has, incidentally, also created a fairly booming business in "digests" of the so-called classics; abridgments which eliminate duplication and windy verbiage from descriptive passages have made reasonably readable volumes out of such monstrously overstuffed works as James Fenimore Cooper's *Leatherstocking Tales.*

The modern author's problem in presenting background is to determine what to include and how to show it. He best solves this problem by remembering his viewpoint position and projecting himself into his viewpoint character's life. From this perspective, his subjective view of what surrounds him is colored by three continuously operating factors: totality of the character, which creates his personality and habit of thought; the emotional state of the character at the time; and the requirements of the dramatic situation or plot.

Totality of character

First, the totality of the character: Let's say our character is contemplating a rolling meadow which is covered by a lush stand of virgin grass. A farmer would see it as a fine place to raise a crop; an architect as a setting for a house; a real estate developer as a prospective location for a subdivision; a cattleman as a place to fatten cattle; a military tactician as a murderous obstacle to taking the next enemy defensive island. The possibilities are limited only by the variety of mankind, and descriptions would vary greatly, depending on the viewpoint of each of these individuals. Probably only a conservationist or an idle, purposeless romantic would see the "lush stand of virgin grass" as such.

Emotional state

It doesn't take much introspective examination to recognize that we see the same thing differently from day to day, depending upon our emotional state at a given time. On the day his college has won a football game and been approved by the regional accrediting association, the college administrator will stand before the memorial bell tower on his campus and hear its chimes as the voice of freedom, ringing out for all to hear. On the next day if the student body riots and the board of trustees decrees that all administrative policies affecting students must have prior approval of the student senate, within the hour that same tower chime can begin to toll the death knell of education.

The requirements of the dramatic situation or plot

control the breadth of the background view. The story should have no more than is necessary to support the viewpoint character's participation and to make the story believable. For example, if that lush rolling meadow had no effect upon the viewpoint character's past and is going to have no significance in his future, a description of it would have no place in the narrative. On the other hand, if the viewpoint character spent his childhood riding horses across that meadow and has now as a part of the story's plot come back to offer his very life if necessary to preserve it as it was, the meadow must be adequately described *in his viewpoint* so the reader will feel it as a sufficiently strong motivating force to move the character. Otherwise, the reader will not be able to understand what all the to-do is about.

Story background is a composite of the time, the place, and the social atmosphere in which the action of the story occurs. The reader wants to know the basic facts of background as soon as possible after beginning the narrative. Sometimes background is his reason for reading, as in the case of many a reader of Westerns. In any event, the reader deserves to know, before he is halfway through the story, that he is reading a period piece set in the Roman Empire.

However, if a story is obviously contemporary and the exact time is of absolutely no import to the characterization and the action, there is no need to go out of one's way to inform the reader of miscellaneous extraneous details concerning the time in which he is living. The geographic aspect of place may or may not be important. For example, a story laid in a hospital in Cairo,

Egypt, could strongly depend upon the geographical location for one's understanding of the characters and the action, while a story in which the action was confined within the walls of a hospital located in Big City, U. S. A., could require not one word about the geographical location if the plot of the story was concerned only with hospital background.

If social atmosphere is of considerable importance to a story, its presentation will in general adequately establish both time and place. A background of social life on a plantation in the Old South—complete with southern belles, southern drawls, and singing slaves —could hardly be presented apart from time and place.

Background should not be plastered on the page in swipes and swirls of words, no matter how well textured, to form a backdrop for the characters' actions. In writing a story, the writer must show the effect of the setting on his characters, and the interaction between these characters and their backgrounds. This cannot be accomplished through the use of solid patches of exposition and description. The writer must show the reaction of the viewpoint character to the background and setting, and let the reader experience this reaction vicariously as it is happening in the story. Let us contrast the two methods:

Bernadine Cosby looked out of the window to see if she needed to carry an umbrella. London was draped with its inevitable veil of dun-colored fog, hanging over its chimney pots like a reflection of the sodden, mud-colored streets beneath. The roofs and chimneys glistened dully, as if slimy, and the fog seemed to run

off them, down into the streets in swirling yellow tentacles to catch passersby, to confuse their direction and
turn their purpose until they could no longer remember where they were going. Its cold clamminess pene-
trated their bodies, making it more important to find
a warm haven than to get where they were going.

Bernadine stepped out of their Gray's Inn flat—
"diggings," as Richard called it—and into the fog. She
carried her green umbrella to match her green shoes
and purse, not that there was any use of trying to dress
up in such weather. She wondered if she had been warm
a single time during the past three years. Well, maybe
once—last night when Driggsby McKeever had told her
about Phoenix, Arizona.

Bernadine crossed Holborn toward Chancery Lane,
where Richard was waiting for her, waiting to spend
another year in this miserable city—all because of his
precious "mission to Britain." She felt the dampness
biting into her. Only last night, while Richard was upholding the future of international law with an Old
Bailey judge, Driggsby had opened the door to warmth
—and back to the United States.

"Bernie, hope of you is the only thing that's keeping
me here now. I've gotten everything I want out of
London. I'd a heap rather write in the sunshine in
Phoenix, with you at my side and people who speak
real English next door."

As she stepped up onto the curb, the fog in Chancery
Lane seemed to form an impenetrable gray between her
and Richard.

To hell with Richard. To hell with international law.
To hell with London and its weather. She continued
down Holborn to Kingsway and Endell Street. She
zigzagged the mews and lanes to Covent Garden Market
—well, really to Phoenix, Arizona. She left London and

its fog behind her as she entered the warmth of Driggsby's tiny room on Bedford Street, London, W.C.2.

The above passage illustrates a common reason for
ineffective writing. The fog doesn't really penetrate
Bernadine. The reader is told about the fog and how it
affects people, and then he is expected to believe that
she leaves Richard in favor of Driggsby because of
London's weather. Contrast that with the following
passage in which the effect of the weather takes place
within the viewpoint character:

Bernadine Cosby looked out of the window to see if
she needed an umbrella, as if there were ever any
doubt in London. Dreary dun-colored fog hung over the
sea of chimney pots. Bernadine picked up the green
umbrella, to match her green shoes and purse, and
headed down the stairs.

She left their Gray's Inn flat—"diggings," as Richard
called it. The fog reached out at her with yellow
tentacles, as if trying to catch her and confuse her. The
clamminess seeped through her, and Bernadine wondered if she had been warm a single time during the
past three years. Well, maybe once—last night when
Driggsby McKeever had told her about Phoenix,
Arizona.

Bernadine stepped off to cross Holborn toward
Chancery Lane where Richard was waiting for her, waiting to spend another year in this miserable city—all because of his precious "mission to Britain." She watched
people looming at her out of the fog as she crossed
Holborn and wondered if anybody in London knew
where he was going. Or were they just wading through
the miserable cold, blindly hoping to find a warm place?

Bernadine stepped up onto the curb. Only last night, while Richard was upholding the future of international law with an Old Bailey judge, Driggsby had opened the door to warmth—and back to the United States.

"Bernie, hope of you is the only thing that's keeping me here now. I've gotten everything I want out of London. I'd a heap rather write in the sunshine in Phoenix, with you at my side and people who speak real English next door."

The fog in Chancery Lane seemed to build into an impenetrable gray wall. Richard's office would be full of it, and so would the restaurant where they would eat lunch. Bernadine drew back, shivering from the coldness of Chancery Lane.

To hell with Richard. To hell with international law. To hell with London. She continued down Holborn to Kingsway and Endell Street. She zigzagged the mews and lanes to Covent Garden Market—well, really to Phoenix, Arizona. She left London's fog swirling behind her as she entered the warmth of Driggsby's tiny room on Bedford Street, London, W.C.2.

Any time the writer is presenting a geographical setting, he should include at least one feature likely to be familiar to the majority of his readers. For example, as a longtime resident of El Paso, Texas, I could write a story laid against its haunts and bypaths, during the course of which I would never mention a detail which would be familiar to the casual visitor. Those equally well acquainted with the city would recognize the authenticity; however, those who had visited casually —tourists, perhaps—would maintain that I didn't know what I was writing about: "Why, I've been to El Paso.

There's a great big mountain with a lot of letters on it sticking right up out of the middle of town. This guy doesn't mention it; he's probably never been there."

In the case of anything which is published for national circulation, there are going to be a lot more readers who are casually acquainted with any location you write about than there will be who know it intimately.

When you go to a new place, particularly a place you are going to stay for some time, it is a good idea for you to capture your first impressions in a notebook for future reference. You see it first as the newcomer or casual visitor sees it, but never again will you have that same view. As you live in a location, the commonplace tends to fade into the background and become unimportant. In your presentation of background, showing or at least mentioning a salient feature—like Old Bailey, Chancery Lane, and chimney pots—will tend to build your reader's confidence in the authenticity of your treatment.

In a story for national publication you must be wary of using background details which are locally common but which would be incomprehensible to, say, the Boston reader. For example, El Paso, Texas, is located across the Rio Grande from Juárez, Mexico. Locally the expression "going across the river" or "across the river" is common colloquial reference to visiting Juárez. There is nothing wrong with using the expression, but it must be translated. The geographical relationship must be established for the majority of readers who haven't any idea of what El Paso, Juárez, and the Rio Grande mean to each other.

A most common difficulty with presenting background comes from failure on the part of the writer to convey to his reader, via viewpoint, the actual mood or effect of the area he is dealing with. This usually results from over-familiarity on the part of the writer. Let's take someone who is intimately acquainted with a particular stretch of Southwestern desert. He might write:

> Don Diego left the waterhole at the beginning of *El Jornada del Muerto,* the Journey of Death, at dawn. The sun was only an hour above the peaks of the San Andreas before he cast aside his heavy helmet . . . and then he shed his breastplates to let the steaming sweat evaporate from his sopping shirtwaist. An hour later he collapsed on the burning sand, gasping through lips that were cracked and bleeding.

To the writer familiar with the effect of the blazing sun on one who would be so hapless as to have to walk this particular stretch of thirst-ridden desert in armor, it is all very meaningful: For him the passage tells of endless soft sand, interspersed with cruel volcanic rocks; slashing cactus; scampering centipedes; searing wind that blinds the eyes and scorches the throat; and above all a hot, glowing ball of fire that never ceases boiling the water from one's body.

But what did he get on paper? The reader, who may never have been west of the Mississippi, learns that somebody took a two-hour walk and keeled over—unlikely, Journey of Death or no Journey of Death. The only conclusion would be that Don Diego must have been in wretched physical condition.

The moral is that the writer must translate his own familiarity with background into an experience which his reader can feel and understand. Viewpoint offers the best vehicle.

Occasionally there comes a time, however, when it is necessary to present background apart from the participation of a viewpoint character, perhaps as an introduction to establish a mood or to present a geographical feature which is going to play a part in the story. Any writer may be tempted to wax eloquent with description. This is fine, as long as he takes the next step: *Cut the description to the minimum necessary to accomplish the task.*

The following example begins with such a description of the Journey of Death which is to be Don Diego's downfall. One could write several thousand descriptive details of this particular stretch of desert, but seventy-five to a hundred carefully chosen words are usually sufficient to set the scene for the viewpoint character. Those words and phrases which contribute to the mood or emotional effect have been italicized. Notice the alternation between fact and feeling:

> The *Journey of Death, El Jornada del Muerto,* spanned twenty-six leagues from the *grassy* bank of the *Rio Grande* to the *glittering* gold under the *forbidding* peaks of the *Fray Cristóbal* range. The *thirst-ridden trace stretched* twice as far as a man could walk from waterhole to waterhole—over *burning* sand *studded* with *slashing* cactus and rocks as *sharp* as *Toledo blades. Centipedes scampered* from rock to rock and *rattlesnakes coiled* in the shade of the cactus.

Don Diego reached the halfway marker against wind that *burned his eyeballs* and *boiled the saliva* from his throat. He *cringed* from the wind to face the *glowing ball* that hung over the San Andreas, turning the armor that protected him from Indian arrows into a *blazing forge* in which a man's courage could be *melted into defeat.*

The *searing* wind split his lip. He *clutched* at the *pain,* and his fingers came away *red, sticky* with the *blood* that ran down into his beard. His helmet *dragged* his chin to his chest, and the *foulness* of his *sweating* body *steamed out* from under his breastplates. He *tore off* his helmet so that he could raise his head and *escape the stench. Sweat trickled* off his eyelids. Through the salty globules, the sun *emblazoned a cross* against the eastern sky.

Don Diego *crossed himself* and his breastplates *burned* his fingertips.

"Caramba! It's *cooking me alive!"*

He *tore away* the straps that held the *Damascus steel* and *flung* it *crashing* to the rocks. The wind went from hot to cold through his shirtwaist.

He *laughed* at a *gasping* lizard and turned toward Fray Cristóbal. The *thrust* of his feet against the *shifting* sand came easier. As the wind took the *life-giving* moisture from his ruffled shirt, the *crags* of the San Andreas turned into a *soft, wavering* line. The rocks and cactus began to dance. The sun *flashed* from a white rock. Don Diego *flinched* from the *glare.* When he turned back toward the *shining* gold, the *Virgin* was looking over the mountain ahead.

He *fell* to his knees and *clutched* the ground, *cool* just beneath the surface.

"Thank God! Oh Virgen querida!"

Don Diego *burrowed* into the *coolness,* away from the sun and into the arms of the *Holy Mother.* The gold of Fray Cristóbal came to him, glancing off the *blinding halo* of his *Lord Jesus*.

You can obtain maximum impact from background description without benefit of character by variety combined with selective moderation. Many elements can contribute to the effect: symbolic names of geographical features ("The Journey of Death"); facts ("centipedes," "rattlesnakes," "trace"); descriptive attributes of the facts ("glittering," "burning," "slashing," "thirst-ridden"); verbs showing what the facts do ("stretched," "coiled," "scampered"); religious or other symbols pertinent to the facts ("Toledo"); contrast—the Journey of Death stretches from a "grassy" river bank across a harsh desert to "forbidding peaks"; familiar landmarks and names which typify the geographical color. (Most readers will have heard of the Rio Grande while *El Jornada del Muerto* and the Fray Crisóbal range communicate the Spanish flavor of the setting.)

The most important thing is to get your viewpoint character into his environment as quickly as possible; have him see, hear, feel, smell, and taste the background around him. Note that the above passage does not use adverbs to describe; a form of the verb "to be" appears only three times in the above 294 words, each time in an auxiliary capacity. The trick is to select details which contribute to—or contrast with—the mood or effect you want. Eliminate everything extraneous. The above passage is somewhat overwritten to provide a greater variety of examples.

Revision

The job of revision can be accomplished in an eleven-step process:

1. Determine the precise mood or emotion you want to communicate. If you can't define the feeling, either the descriptive passage has no place in the narrative or you haven't yet clearly defined its purpose.

2. Go through your description and blue-pencil every single detail which does not contribute to the effect you are striving for. This will leave you with certain facts and words which establish the mood or feeling.

3. Eliminate every fact for which you do not have an associated feeling and every "feeling" phrase or word for which you do not have a supporting fact.

4. Then hammer what you have left into a continuous flow of narrative in which fact and feeling alternate. To check the rhythm of your story, underline once each word or phrase which presents facts, and twice, each word or phrase which establishes feeling. Do not underline those words to which you cannot assign one purpose or the other.

5. Examine every word which is not underlined; each should either be removed or replaced. For example, you may find that you have used a preponderance of forms of the verb "to be." "Is," "are," "was," "were," and all of their derivative forms are lifeless grammatical equal signs. They

lie upon the page, lacking movement and force. Passive verbs are likewise dubious; they connote something *being done* to someone instead of someone *doing* something.

6. Examine all nouns (facts) accompanied by modifying adjectives to give the associated feeling. If you can cut the adjective and substitute for the noun a more precise word which communicates the feeling as a part of the fact, do so.

7. Examine every verb which is accompanied by an adverb. If you can eliminate the adverb and use a more precise verb, do so.

8. Examine every adjective which is accompanied by an adverb. If you can remove the adverb and use a more precise adjective, do so. Note that "very" is one of the weakest words in the English language. No one has yet been able to define the height of a *very* high mountain.

9. Examine every combination of two or more adjectives modifying the same word. The use of two adjectives usually means that the writer has not selected the right one in the first place.

10. Examine all words to see that you are not tending to nullify the effect of the mood you are trying to create by the use of negative forms. For example, let's say you are trying to communicate the fact that the cold of the Antarctic is too severe for life to withstand. If you use the phrase "unbearable cold" you will be introducing along with the word "unbearable" some connotation of the word "bearable," the opposite of the mean-

ing you wish to impart. This means the reader may have to leave the forward progress of his reading to look back for the meaning.

11. Again, hammer what you have left into a flow of fact and feeling. Note in the process that movement can be imparted, even to static things, by the use of word forms ending in "-ing." Such words tend to give an effect of movement simply by their flowing, moving, ringing sounds.

You may consider this process excessively hard labor, but if you follow it conscientiously, you will turn your descriptive material into short, crisp passages. Neither you nor the reader will ever be in doubt about what you are trying to say or the effect you are trying to create. And, best of all, eventually you will find your first drafts improving.